SQUARE DEAL

SQUARE

DEAL

Easy Quilts from Squares and Rectangles

NANCY MAHONEY

Martingale®
& COMPANY

Square Deal: Easy Quilts from Squares and Rectangles
© 2007 by Nancy Mahoney

That Patchwork Place® is an imprint
of Martingale & Company®.

Martingale & Company
20205 144th Ave. NE
Woodinville, WA 98072-8478
www.martingale-pub.com

Printed in China
12 11 10 09 08 07   8 7 6 5 4 3 2 1

Library of Congress Cataloging-in-Publication Data
Library of Congress Control Number: 2006035735

ISBN: 978-1-56477-718-8

Credits

CEO: Tom Wierzbicki
Publisher: Jane Hamada
Editorial Director: Mary V. Green
Managing Editor: Tina Cook
Technical Editor: Laurie Bevan
Copy Editor: Melissa Bryan
Design Director: Stan Green
Illustrators: Wendy Slotboom and Laurel Strand
Text Designer: Trina Craig
Cover Designer: Stan Green
Photographer: Brent Kane

Mission Statement

*Dedicated to providing quality
products and service to
inspire creativity.*

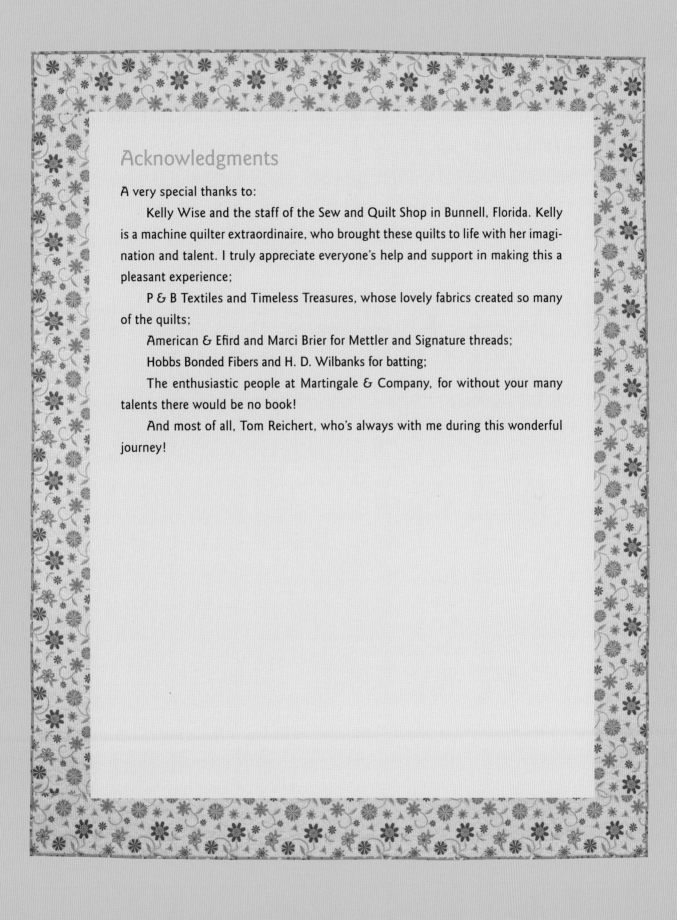

Acknowledgments

A very special thanks to:

Kelly Wise and the staff of the Sew and Quilt Shop in Bunnell, Florida. Kelly is a machine quilter extraordinaire, who brought these quilts to life with her imagination and talent. I truly appreciate everyone's help and support in making this a pleasant experience;

P & B Textiles and Timeless Treasures, whose lovely fabrics created so many of the quilts;

American & Efird and Marci Brier for Mettler and Signature threads;

Hobbs Bonded Fibers and H. D. Wilbanks for batting;

The enthusiastic people at Martingale & Company, for without your many talents there would be no book!

And most of all, Tom Reichert, who's always with me during this wonderful journey!

CONTENTS

Keys to SUCCESS

During my wonderful journey as a quilter, I have made many quilts that reflect a variety of styles and use a variety of techniques. As my life has changed, so has my approach to quiltmaking. As an author and quilt designer, I need to make lots of quilts every year—would you believe 40 to 50 quilts a year? Many of the quilts are lap size or larger, and over the past few months, at least two have been queen size. I'm sure you're wondering how this is possible, which brings me to the reason for this book. I love to use traditional patterns, but with a new twist. For this book, I've designed 16 simple patterns, all using my quick and easy approach to quiltmaking. In this section I've listed some of my favorite and most valuable timesaving tips.

Advance planning. Knowing that time is always a factor, I carefully plan each quilt. I start by using my computer to determine the layout. With software designed for quilting, you can try different blocks, add sashing (plain or pieced), add borders, and play with fabric selection, all at the press of a key. All the quilts in *Square Deal* started on my computer.

Large blocks. An easy approach to making large quilts quickly is to use large blocks. One way to make a block larger is to add a frame of squares and rectangles around the center block or unit. In "Stepping Out" on page 33, I used this technique to make the finished blocks 16" rather than 12". The key is to make sure the frame blends with the center block or unit.

Sashing strips. I have come to truly appreciate the role sashing strips can play in the design of a quilt. When I first began making quilts, I usually set the blocks side by side to create a secondary pattern. As I've become more experienced at quiltmaking, I've discovered you can create exciting secondary designs with sashing—either pieced or plain. Sashing also makes sewing the blocks together easier. Not only is this a time-saver, but you also don't have to worry about matching the block seams between the rows.

I love to use traditional patterns, but with a new twist.

Fabric selection. Quilts are much easier and faster to make if you use a limited number of fabrics in each project, because you'll have fewer fabrics to handle and cut. When using a limited number of fabrics, each fabric takes on a more important role in your quilt, so each should be appealing and have enough contrast. You can still make scrappy-looking quilts, but your fabric choices will be more limited. Instead of using 25 to 30 red fabrics, select 3 or 4 red prints as I did in "Square Crossing" on page 69. A scrappy look can make a simple design more interesting. Fabric selection can be a long ordeal, but it doesn't need to be. Start with a theme or focal piece; this is usually a large-scale multicolored print that can be used in the outer border. Then select other fabrics that blend with, match, or complement the theme or focal fabric. The number of fabrics you select will depend on the quilt you are making. I usually pull out more fabrics than I'll need and eliminate the ones I don't like or that aren't working.

Sewing tips. To make the most of my sewing time, I use efficient piecing techniques whenever possible. In "Quiltmaking Basics," beginning on page 10, you will find the details for the many timesaving piecing methods that are used to make the quilts in this book.

The time devoted to designing your quilt and selecting the fabrics will be well spent. If all the decisions are made during the design stage, constructing the quilt becomes a quick and easy process. However, keep an open mind. Make one block to test your fabric selection; if something isn't working the way you want, making the changes now will save time in the end.

Like most of you, although my time is limited, I have broad tastes that change with my mood. So there's sure to be something for everyone in this diverse collection. I hope you have as much fun making these quilts as I have. You just need to decide which one to make first!

Quiltmaking BASICS

On the pages that follow, you will find valuable information to help you with the successful completion of your quilt. All of the special techniques needed are covered in this section.

Rotary Cutting

Instructions for rotary cutting are provided for all the quilts, and *all rotary-cutting measurements include ¼"-wide seam allowances.* If you're unfamiliar with rotary cutting, refer to *The Quilter's Quick Reference Guide* by Candace Eisner Strick (Martingale & Company, 2004) for more detailed rotary-cutting instructions. Basic rotary-cutting tools include a rotary cutter, an 18" x 24" cutting mat, a 6" x 24" acrylic ruler, and a 6" Bias Square®, which you will use for some of the sew-and-trim techniques described in this section. It is also very useful for making cleanup cuts and for crosscutting squares and rectangles. You'll be able to make all the projects in this book with these rulers. Note that rotary-cutting instructions are written for right-handers; reverse the instructions if you are left-handed.

Cutting Strips

It is essential that you cut strips at an exact right angle to the folded edge of your fabric. Rotary cutting squares, rectangles, and other shapes begins with cutting accurate strips.

Press the fabric, and then fold it in half with the selvages together. Place the fabric on your cutting mat with the folded edge nearest to your body. Align a Bias Square with the fold of the fabric and

place a 6" x 24" ruler to the left so that the raw edges of the fabric are covered.

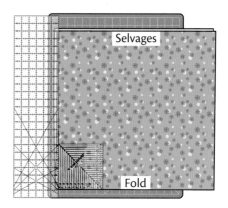

Remove the square ruler and make a rotary cut along the right edge of the long ruler. Remove the long ruler and gently remove the waste strip. This is called a cleanup cut.

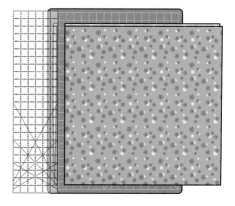

Align the desired strip width on the ruler with the cut edge of the fabric, and carefully cut a strip. After cutting three or four strips, realign the square ruler along the fold and make a new cleanup cut if necessary. Continue cutting until you have the required number of strips.

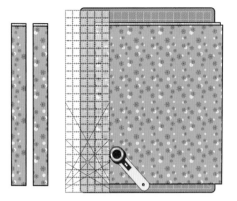

Cutting Squares and Rectangles

To cut squares and rectangles, cut a strip in the desired width and carefully remove the selvage ends by making a cleanup cut. Align the desired measurements on the ruler (or Bias Square) with the left edge of the strip and cut a square or rectangle. Continue cutting until you have the required number of pieces.

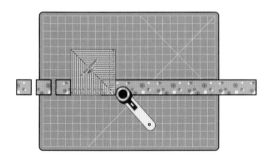

Sew-and-Trim Techniques

Sew-and-trim techniques make use of strips, rectangles, and squares that are sewn together and trimmed to create units for the blocks. Admittedly, these techniques do require a little more fabric than other methods because some of the fabric gets trimmed away in the end, but most quilters find the improved accuracy worth it. These techniques are handy for a variety of common patchwork units. Once you try this method, you'll be surprised how many uses you'll find for it.

Making Strip Sets

Strip sets consist of two or more long strips of fabric that are sewn together and then crosscut into smaller segments of squares or rectangles. Strip sets are a quick, efficient, and accurate way of cutting and piecing blocks and block units.

1. Cut the specific number of strips in the required width for the quilt you are making. Arrange the strips in the correct color combinations. With right sides together, sew the strips together along the long edges. Press the seams as indicated.

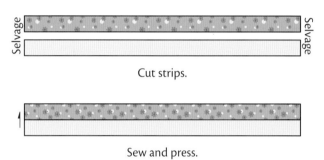

Cut strips.

Sew and press.

2. Square up the ends of the strip set to remove the selvages. Align the required measurement on the ruler with the cleanly cut left edge of the strip set, and cut the specified number of segments. After cutting a few segments, check that your cuts are at right angles to the sewn seam, and square up if needed. This step of checking and retrimming is necessary because slight stretching of the strips may occur during sewing.

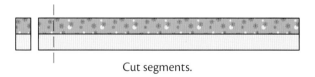

Cut segments.

Square-on-Square Units

Many of the quilts in this book feature blocks made with the following technique. This is a wonderful way of creating triangles without actually cutting triangles and sewing on the bias.

1. Cut squares the sizes specified in the cutting list. Draw a diagonal line from corner to corner on the wrong side of the smaller squares as directed.

2. With right sides together, position the squares on the larger square as directed in the quilt instructions. Sew along the corner side of the drawn line. Sewing next to the line compensates for the slight inaccuracy caused during pressing of the unit.

    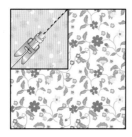

3. Trim away the excess fabric, leaving a ¼" seam allowance. Press the seams as specified in the project instructions.

    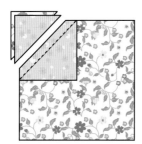

Depending on how the squares are combined, you can make a variety of units.

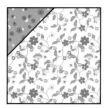

Square sewn on one corner

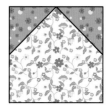
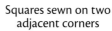
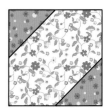

Squares sewn on two adjacent corners

Squares sewn on two opposite corners

Square-and-Rectangle Units

This technique is used to make many of the blocks in this book. All you do is cut squares and stitch them to a rectangle.

1. Cut squares the size specified in the cutting list. Draw a diagonal line from corner to corner on the wrong side of the squares as directed.

2. With right sides together, position a square on the rectangle as directed in the quilt instructions. Begin sewing at the center of the rectangle, with your stitching line skimming along the corner side of the drawn line. Starting to sew in the middle of the rectangle helps keep the needle from pushing the fabric down into the bobbin hole. Sewing next to the line compensates for the slight inaccuracy caused during pressing of the unit.

3. Trim away the excess fabric, leaving a ¼" seam allowance. Press the seams as specified in the project instructions.

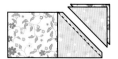 

Square sewn on one end of rectangle

Squares sewn on both ends of rectangle

Squares sewn on opposite corners of rectangle

Rectangle-to-Rectangle Units

Here's a great technique that eliminates the need for templates. You'll start with two or three rectangles.

1. Cut rectangles the size specified in the cutting list. Working on the wrong side of one of the rectangles, align the 45° line of your Bias Square with a long edge of the fabric piece and draw a diagonal line as directed. If you are creating units of three rectangles sewn together, the seam of the second rectangle will need to be sewn in the opposite direction of the first one. In this case, you'll need to mark half of the rectangles with the diagonal slanting to the left and the other half with the diagonal slanting to the right.

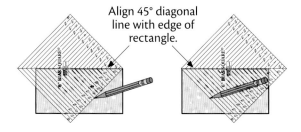

Align 45° diagonal line with edge of rectangle.

2. With right sides together, position a marked rectangle on top of the base rectangle, lining up the corners as shown. Stitch along the corner side of the drawn line. Sewing next to the line compensates for the slight inaccuracy caused during pressing of the unit.

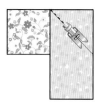

3. Trim away the excess fabric, leaving a ¼" seam allowance. Press the seam as indicated in the project instructions.

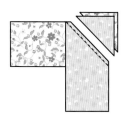

Two rectangles sewn together

Three rectangles sewn together

Three rectangles sewn together

Flying-Geese Units

Several of the blocks in this book contain flying-geese units. The following steps describe a quick and easy method for making these units using squares and rectangles.

1. Cut squares the size specified in the cutting list. Draw a diagonal line from corner to corner on the wrong side of the squares as directed.

2. Position a marked square on one corner of a large rectangle, right sides together and raw edges aligned. Stitch along the corner side of the drawn line. Sewing next to the line compensates for the slight inaccuracy caused during pressing of the unit. Trim away the excess fabric, leaving a ¼" seam allowance. Press the seam toward the triangle.

 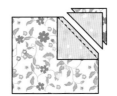

3. Repeat for each corner.

4. Align your ruler so that the ¼" mark is on one set of crossed seams and the 45° diagonal line is along the seam line. Using your rotary cutter, cut along the edge of the ruler to make one flying-geese unit.

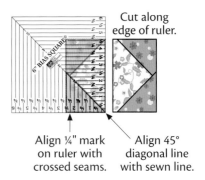

Cut along edge of ruler.

Align ¼" mark on ruler with crossed seams.

Align 45° diagonal line with sewn line.

5. Repeat step 4 with the other half of the large rectangle, realigning your ruler and cutting along the edge to make a second flying-geese unit.

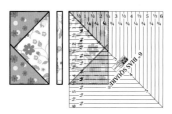

Two flying-geese units

Parallelogram Units

Sew-and-trim techniques can be used to make a parallelogram, which appears in several projects including "Summer Stars" on page 82. Instead of sewing the second square in the opposite direction of the first one, sew the stitching line in the same diagonal direction. Note that a left-leaning parallelogram is the reverse of a right-leaning parallelogram, and they are not interchangeable. If you need both types, you'll need to stitch some shapes with lines slanting left and some with lines slanting right.

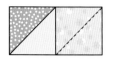 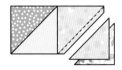

Parallelogram unit   Reverse parallelogram unit

Pressing

Pressing is one of the keys to precise piecing. It is important to carefully press your work after stitching each seam. Set your iron on the cotton setting and use a padded pressing surface to prevent the seam allowance from creating a ridge on the right side of the unit. Use a pressing cloth when ironing raised areas with multiple seams. (This protects your fabrics from becoming glazed and shiny under the iron.) To avoid possible distortion, allow the pieces to cool before moving them from the pressing surface.

Long Seams

When pressing long seams, first press the seam flat from the wrong side to smooth out any puckers. To avoid stretching the fabric, use an up-and-down motion rather than the back-and-forth, gliding motion typical of ironing. Open the sewn unit and, from the right side, press in the direction indicated in the project diagram. Use the tip of the iron to gently push the fabric over the seam.

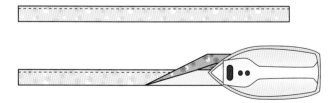

Four-Patch Units

When pressing four-patch units, or other blocks and block units that join four fabric pieces, you can create opposing seams and reduce bulk where the four seams meet. After the seam is sewn, use a seam ripper to remove one or two stitches from the seam allowance. Gently reposition the seam allowances to evenly distribute the fabric. Press the seam allowances in opposite directions.

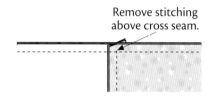

Remove stitching above cross seam.

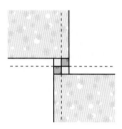

Back of a four-patch unit

Assembling the QUILT TOP

After you have made all the blocks, cut or made the sashing, and cut setting pieces as needed, you are ready to assemble the quilt top as directed for your specific project.

Quilts with Blocks
Set Side by Side

1. Arrange the blocks in rows as shown in the assembly diagram for your project.

2. Sew the blocks together in horizontal rows. Press the seams in opposite directions from one row to the next, unless instructed otherwise. If you are alternating plain blocks with pieced blocks, press all the seams toward the plain blocks.

3. Pin the rows together, being careful to match the seams from row to row. Sew the rows together and press the seams all in one direction unless instructed otherwise.

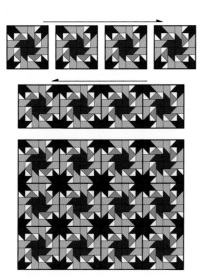

Quilt with blocks set side by side

Quilts with Sashing Strips

For quilts with sashing strips or units, measure the blocks (including seam allowance) and trim the sashing units as needed to match the block measurement. Follow the assembly diagrams for your project to arrange the blocks, sashing strips, and corner squares, if applicable. Join the blocks and vertical sashing strips into rows, pressing the seams toward the sashing strips. Join the horizontal sashing strips and corner squares into rows, once again pressing toward the sashing strips. Sew the rows together and press the seams toward the sashing unit/corner square rows.

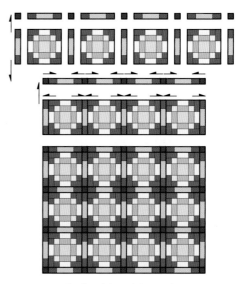

Quilt with sashing units
and corner squares

Two of the quilts in this book are made without corner squares. The blocks in each horizontal row are separated by vertical sashing strips. Then the rows of blocks are separated by long sashing strips that extend from side to side across the quilt top. Measure the completed block rows and trim the long sashing strips to match that measurement.

When the block rows and long sashing strips are sewn together, it's important for the short vertical sashing strips to correctly line up on each side of the long sashing strip. One easy way to make the strips line up is to mark the long strips with pins to show the junctions that must match. Join the rows, matching the seam junctions with the pins. Press the seam allowances toward the long sashing strips.

Quilt with long sashing strips

Quilts Set Diagonally

The blocks for diagonal settings are placed on point and arranged in diagonal rows. Setting triangles are then added to fill in the side and corner spaces.

1. Arrange the blocks, sashing units (if applicable), setting triangles, and corner triangles as shown in the quilt assembly diagram for your project.

2. Sew the blocks, sashing units (if applicable), and side setting triangles together in diagonal rows; press the seams toward the sashing units.

3. Sew the rows together, matching the seams from row to row. Press as directed in the

project instructions. Sew the corner triangles on last and press toward these triangles.

Quilt set diagonally

Borders

Most quilts have a border or borders that frame the pieced blocks. Borders can be simple strips of one or more fabrics. They can also be pieced or appliquéd and used in combination with plain strips.

Prepare border strips a few inches longer than you'll actually need; then trim them to the correct length once you know the dimensions of the center of your quilt top. To find the correct measurement for the border strips, always measure through the center of the quilt, not at the outside edges. This ensures that the borders are of equal length on opposite sides of the quilt and helps keep your quilt square.

Borders wider than 2" are usually cut on the lengthwise grain (parallel to the selvage) so that they don't stretch and don't have to be pieced. You'll save fabric if you attach the borders to the longer sides of the quilt top first, and then attach them to the remaining two sides.

For quilts smaller than 40" square, or if you do not have enough fabric to cut the strips from the lengthwise grain, strips cut on the crosswise grain (across the fabric from selvage to selvage) work perfectly fine.

TIMELY TIPS

When assembling the quilt top, you may discover that blocks or blocks and borders intended to match may vary slightly in size. To ease the pieces together, pin the ends, the points to match, and in between as needed to distribute the excess fabric. Sew with the shortest piece on top; the action of the feed dogs will ease the fullness of the bottom piece.

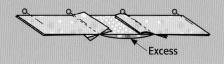

Excess

Borders less than 2" wide are usually cut from the crosswise grain and joined end to end with a diagonal seam to achieve the required length. This is the most fabric-efficient way to cut narrow border strips.

Measuring for Length of Border Strips

1. Measure the length of the quilt top from top to bottom through the center. Cut two border strips to this measurement, piecing as necessary.

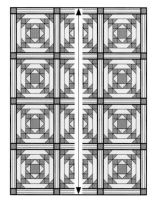

Measure the center of the quilt, top to bottom.

2. Mark the center of the border strips and the center of the sides of the quilt top. Pin the borders to the sides of the quilt top, matching

centers and ends. Ease or slightly stretch the quilt top to fit the border strip as necessary. Sew the side borders in place with a ¼"-wide seam and press the seams toward the border strips.

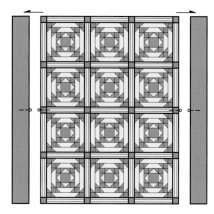

Mark centers.

3. Measure the width of the quilt top from side to side through the center (including the side borders just added) to determine the length of the top and bottom border strips. Cut two strips to this measurement, piecing as necessary. Mark the center of the border strips and the center of the top and bottom of the quilt top. Pin the borders to the quilt top, matching centers and ends. Ease or slightly stretch the quilt to fit the border strips as necessary. Sew the borders in place with a ¼"-wide seam and press the seams toward the border strips.

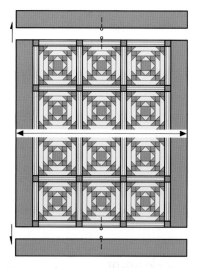

Measure the center of the quilt, side to side, including the borders. Mark centers.

Finishing Your QUILT

Quilts consist of three layers—the quilt top, backing, and batting. Now that your quilt top is done, you're ready to move on to the finishing stages.

Backing and Batting

For the quilt backing, cut a piece of fabric 4" to 6" larger than the quilt top (2" to 3" on all sides). For quilts wider than the width of your fabric, you'll need to piece the backing. For most quilts in this book, I've listed enough backing fabric to piece the backing with one seam, allowing an adequate amount of leftover fabric to cut a hanging sleeve. When piecing the backing, be sure to trim off the selvages before sewing the pieces together. Press the seam open to reduce the bulk.

There are many types of batting to choose from. The type of batting you choose will depend on whether you plan to hand or machine quilt your quilt top. New battings are always being developed, so check with your favorite quilt shop for the most recent products. Generally, the thinner the batting—whether cotton or polyester—the easier it is to hand quilt. For machine quilting, a cotton batting works best. It won't move or slip between the quilt top and backing. Whatever type of batting you choose, the piece should be large enough to allow an extra 2" around all edges of the quilt top.

Layering and Quilting Your Quilt

Before you layer the quilt, give the quilt top and backing a careful pressing. Then spread the backing, wrong side up, on a flat, clean surface. Anchor

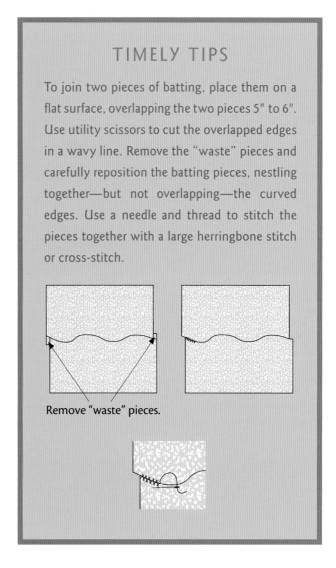

TIMELY TIPS

To join two pieces of batting, place them on a flat surface, overlapping the two pieces 5" to 6". Use utility scissors to cut the overlapped edges in a wavy line. Remove the "waste" pieces and carefully reposition the batting pieces, nestling together—but not overlapping—the curved edges. Use a needle and thread to stitch the pieces together with a large herringbone stitch or cross-stitch.

Remove "waste" pieces.

the backing with pins or masking tape, taking care not to stretch the fabric out of shape. Center the batting over the backing, smoothing out any wrinkles. Center the pressed quilt top, right side up, over the batting, smoothing out any wrinkles and making sure the edges of the quilt top are parallel to the edges of the backing. Note that you should always smooth outward from the center and along straight lines to ensure that the blocks and borders remain straight.

For hand quilting, baste with needle and thread, starting in the center of the quilt and working diagonally to each corner. Continue basting in a grid of horizontal and vertical lines 6" to 8" apart. To finish, baste around the edges about 1/8" from the edge of the quilt top.

For machine quilting, baste the layers with size #2 rustproof safety pins. Place pins 4" to 6" apart; try to avoid areas where you intend to quilt. Finish by machine basting around the edges about 1/8" from the edge of the quilt top.

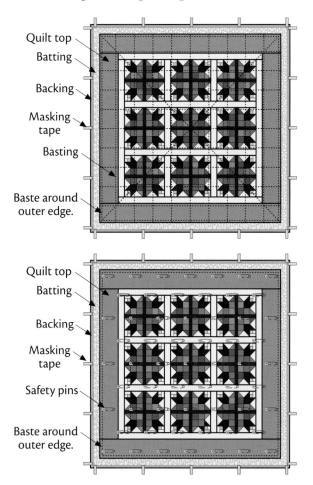

As a general rule, no unquilted areas should exceed 4" x 4". In addition, check the package of the batting that you are using for recommendations concerning the appropriate amount of quilting. The density of your quilting should be similar throughout the entire quilt so that the quilt will remain square and will not become distorted.

To quilt by hand, you will need short, sturdy needles (called "Betweens"), quilting thread, and a thimble to fit the middle finger of your sewing hand. Most quilters use a frame or hoop to support their work. For excellent guidance regarding all aspects of hand-quilting techniques, see *Loving Stitches: A Guide to Fine Hand Quilting, Revised Edition* by Jeana Kimball (Martingale & Company, 2003).

Machine quilting is suitable for all types and sizes of quilts and allows you to complete a quilt quickly. For straight-line quilting, a walking foot is extremely helpful for feeding the layers through the machine without shifting or puckering. For free-motion quilting, you need a darning foot and the ability to drop the feed dogs on your machine. With free-motion quilting, you don't turn the fabric under the needle but instead guide the fabric in the direction of the design. Because the feed dogs are lowered, the stitch length is determined by the speed at which you run the machine and feed the fabric under the foot. For more information on machine quilting, refer to *Machine Quilting Made Easy* by Maurine Noble (Martingale & Company, 1994).

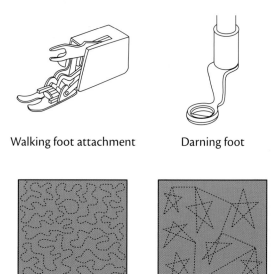

Walking foot attachment   Darning foot

Squaring Up Your Quilt

When you complete the quilting, you'll need to trim the excess backing and batting as well as square up your quilt before sewing on the binding. Make sure all the basting thread or pins have been removed, but leave the basting stitches around the outer edges. Align a ruler with the seam line of the outer border and measure the width of the outer border in several places. Using the narrowest measurement, position a ruler along the seam line of the outer border and trim the excess batting and backing from all four sides. Use a large, square ruler to square up each corner.

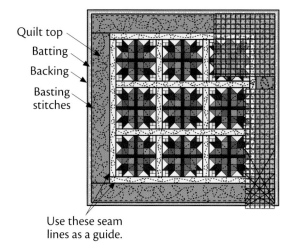

Quilt top
Batting
Backing
Basting
stitches

Use these seam
lines as a guide.

Making a Hanging Sleeve

If you plan to hang the finished quilt, attach a hanging sleeve or rod pocket to the back now, before you bind the quilt.

From the leftover backing fabric, cut an 8"-wide strip of fabric equal to the width of your quilt. On each short end of the strip, fold over ½" and then fold ½" again to make a hem. Press and stitch by machine.

Fold the strip in half lengthwise, wrong sides together; baste the raw edges to the top edge of the back of your quilt. These raw edges will be secured when you sew on the binding. Your quilt should be about 1" wider than the sleeve on both sides.

Make a little pleat in the sleeve to accommodate the thickness of the rod, and then slipstitch the ends and bottom edge of the sleeve to the backing fabric. This keeps the rod from being inserted next to the quilt backing.

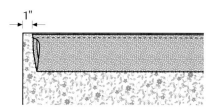

1"

Binding Your Quilt

The binding offers a wonderful opportunity to add to the overall look of your quilt. If you want the binding to "disappear," use the same fabric for the binding as for the outer border. If you want the binding to frame the outer border or act as an additional border, select a fabric that is different from the outer border.

Strips for binding are generally cut 2" to 2½" wide, depending on your preference for binding width and your choice of batting. (I used 2"-wide strips for the quilts in this book.) Cut enough strips to go around the perimeter of your quilt plus about 10" extra for making seams and turning corners.

1. To make one long, continuous strip, piece the strips at right angles and stitch across the corner as shown. Trim the excess fabric, leaving a ¼"-wide seam, and press the seams open.

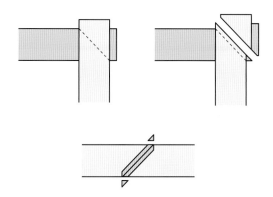

2. Cut one end of the long binding strip at a 45° angle. Press the strip in half lengthwise, wrong sides together and raw edges aligned.

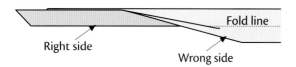

Right side

Fold line

Wrong side

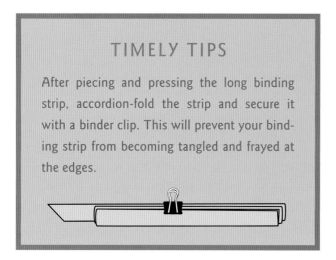

TIMELY TIPS

After piecing and pressing the long binding strip, accordion-fold the strip and secure it with a binder clip. This will prevent your binding strip from becoming tangled and frayed at the edges.

3. Beginning with the angled end of the binding strip, align the raw edge of the strip with the raw edge of the quilt. Starting on the bottom edge of the quilt (not at a corner), and beginning 8" from the strip's angled end, use a walking foot and a ¼"-wide seam to stitch the binding strip to the quilt. Stop ¼" from the first corner and backstitch.

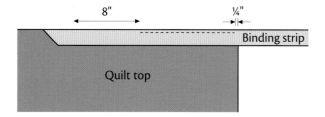

8"   ¼"

Binding strip

Quilt top

4. Remove the quilt from the sewing machine. Fold the binding up and away from the quilt at a 45° angle, and then fold down again and pin as shown to create an angled pleat at the corner. Begin with a backstitch at the fold of the binding and continue stitching along the edge of the quilt top, mitering each corner as you come to it.

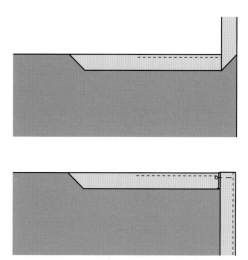

5. Stop stitching approximately 12" from the starting end of the binding strip and backstitch. Remove the quilt from the machine. Place the quilt on a flat surface and layer the beginning (angled) tail on top of the ending tail. Mark the ending tail where it meets the beginning tail. Make a second mark ½" to the right of the first mark.

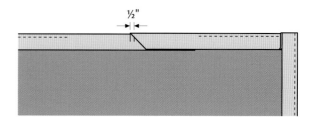

½"

6. Open the ending tail strip and align the 45° line of a small Bias Square with the top edge of the opened binding strip. Place the corner of the ruler on the second mark. Cut the ending tail strip along the edge of the ruler as shown. The ends of both binding strips will form 45° angles and overlap ½".

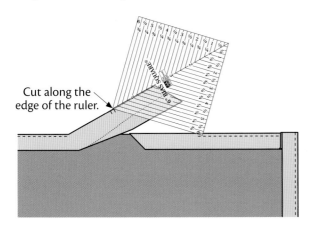

Cut along the edge of the ruler.

7. Place the binding ends right sides together, aligning the angled raw edges as shown. Fold the quilt out of the way and stitch the ends together using a ¼" seam allowance. Press the seam open, refold the binding, and then press the fold. Then finish stitching the binding to the quilt top.

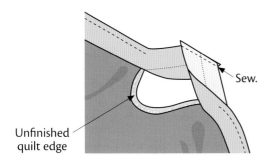

Sew.

Unfinished quilt edge

8. Turn the binding to the back of the quilt. Using thread to match the binding, hand stitch the binding in place so that the folded edge covers the row of machine stitching. At each corner, fold the binding to form a miter on the back of the quilt.

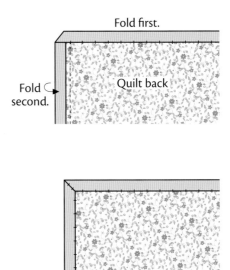

Fold first.

Fold second.

Quilt back

Adding a Label

A label provides important information including the name of the quilt, the person who made it, and when and where the quilt was made. You may also want to include the name of the recipient, if the quilt is a gift, and any other interesting or important information about the quilt. A label can be as elaborate or as simple as you desire. You can sign your name on the back of the finished quilt using a permanent marker, purchase pretty labels that are printed on fabric, or make your own label.

Blooming PINWHEELS

Simple spinning pinwheels combined with pieced sashing generate an undulating design that dances around this marvelous quilt. The inner border blends with the blocks and sashing to create the look of a scalloped border, so while this looks fairly complex, the piecing is really very easy.

Finished Quilt Size: 48½" x 57½"
Finished Block Size: 8"

Materials

Yardages are based on 42″-wide fabrics.

1½ yards of floral print for outer border and binding
1⅜ yards of cream tonal print for blocks and sashing
1 yard of green tonal print for blocks, sashing, and inner border
¾ yard of red tonal print for blocks
½ yard of gold tonal print for blocks, sashing corners, and middle border
¼ yard of black print for blocks
3¼ yards of fabric for backing
53" x 62" piece of batting

Cutting

All measurements include ¼″-wide seam allowances. Cut all strips across the width of the fabric (selvage to selvage) unless instructed otherwise.

From the cream tonal print, cut:
7 strips, 4½" x 42"; crosscut *5 strips* into 80 rectangles, 2½" x 4½"
5 strips, 2½" x 42"; crosscut into 80 squares, 2½" x 2½"

From the gold tonal print, cut:
3 strips, 2½" x 42"; crosscut into 40 squares, 2½" x 2½"

1 strip, 1½" x 42"; crosscut into 12 squares, 1½" x 1½"
5 strips, 1¼" x 42"

From the red tonal print, cut:
5 strips, 4½" x 42"; crosscut into 80 rectangles, 2½" x 4½"

From the black print, cut:
3 strips, 2½" x 42"; crosscut into 40 squares, 2½" x 2½"

From the green tonal print, cut:
9 strips, 2½" x 42"; crosscut *5 strips* into 80 squares, 2½" x 2½"
5 strips, 1½" x 42"

From the *lengthwise grain* of the floral print, cut:
4 strips, 5½" x 51"
5 strips, 2" x 45"

Making the Blocks

1. Using the parallelogram-unit technique on page 14, draw a diagonal line from corner to corner on the wrong side of the 2½" cream squares and 2½" gold squares. Stitch a cream square and a gold square to a red rectangle as shown. Press as indicated. Make 40. You'll use the remaining marked cream squares in the next step.

Make 40.

2. Draw a diagonal line from corner to corner on the wrong side of the 2½" black squares. Repeat step 1 to sew a black square and one of the remaining marked cream squares to a remaining red rectangle as shown. Press as indicated. Make 40.

Make 40.

3. Using the square-and-rectangle-unit technique on page 12, draw a diagonal line from corner to corner on the wrong side of the 2½" green squares. Sew a green square to one end of a cream rectangle as shown; press. Make 80.

Make 80.

4. Sew one unit from step 1 and one unit from step 3 together as shown to make unit A; press. Make 40.

Unit A.
Make 40.

5. Sew one unit from step 2 and one unit from step 3 together as shown to make unit B; press. Make 40.

Unit B.
Make 40.

6. Sew two of unit A and two of unit B together as shown to make one block; press. Refer to "Four-Patch Units" on page 15 for guidance on positioning and pressing the center seam allowance. Make 20 blocks.

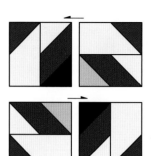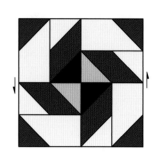

Make 20.

Assembling the Quilt Top

For detailed instructions, refer to "Quilts with Sashing Strips" on page 16.

1. Refer to "Making Strip Sets" on page 11. Sew one 4½" x 42" cream strip between two 2½" x 42" green strips to make a strip set. Press toward the green strips. Make two. Cut the strip sets into 1½"-wide segments. Cut 31 segments.

Make 2 strip sets.
Cut 31 segments.

2. Arrange and sew together three segments from step 1 and four blocks, alternating them as shown to make a block row; press. Make five rows.

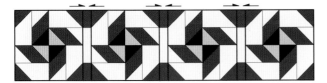

Make 5.

3. Arrange and sew together four segments from step 1 and three 1½" gold squares as shown to make a sashing row; press. Make four rows.

Make 4.

4. Sew the block rows and sashing rows together, alternating them as shown in the assembly diagram. Press the seams toward the sashing rows.

Assembly diagram

5. Refer to "Borders" on page 17. Measure, cut, and sew the 1½"-wide green inner-border strips, then the 1¼"-wide gold middle-border strips, and lastly the 5½"-wide floral outer-border strips to the quilt top.

Finishing the Quilt

For detailed instructions on the following techniques, refer to "Finishing Your Quilt" on page 19.

1. Cut and piece the backing fabric so that it is 4" to 6" larger than the quilt top. Layer the quilt top with batting and backing. Baste the layers together.

2. Hand or machine quilt as desired. You may wish to quilt a medallion in the center of the blocks and a smaller medallion over the sashing corners. Quilt a continuous loop over the inner and middle borders and a continuous design in the outer border.

3. Square up the quilt sandwich.

4. Add a hanging sleeve, if desired.

5. Using the 2"-wide floral strips, sew the binding to the quilt. Add a label, if desired.

Cross ROADS

The bright and bold fabrics in this quick-and-easy checkerboard design create an eye-catching quilt. The simple design and manageable size make this is an ideal project to whip up in a weekend.

Finished Quilt Size: 72" x 72"
Finished Block Size: 12"

Materials

Yardages are based on 42˝-wide fabrics.

2¼ yards of black floral print for outer border

1⅝ yards of red-and-black stripe for sashing and binding

⅞ yard of black-with-circles print for blocks and sashing corners

⅝ yard of white print for blocks

⅝ yard of red tonal print for blocks

⅝ yard of black-and-white print for blocks and sashing corners

⅝ yard of yellow tonal print for blocks and inner border

4½ yards of fabric for backing

76" x 76" piece of batting

Cutting

All measurements include ¼˝-wide seam allowances. Cut all strips across the width of the fabric (selvage to selvage) unless instructed otherwise.

From the yellow tonal print, cut:
4 strips, 2½" x 42"
6 strips, 1¼" x 42"

From the black-and-white print, cut:
7 strips, 2½" x 42"; crosscut *1 strip* into 12 squares, 2½" x 2½"

From the red tonal print, cut:
2 strips, 4½" x 42"
4 strips, 2½" x 42"; crosscut into 32 rectangles, 2½" x 4½"

From the black-with-circles print, cut:
2 strips, 6½" x 42"; crosscut into 32 rectangles, 2½" x 6½"
5 strips, 2½" x 42"; crosscut *1 strip* into 13 squares, 2½" x 2½"

From the white print, cut:
4 strips, 4½" x 42"

From the red-and-black stripe, cut:
14 strips, 2½" x 42"; crosscut into 40 rectangles, 2½" x 12½"
8 strips, 2" x 42"

From the *lengthwise grain* of the black floral print, cut:
4 strips, 6¾" x 75"

Making the Blocks

Refer to "Making Strip Sets" on page 11, if needed.

1. Sew one 2½" x 42" yellow strip and one 2½" x 42" black-and-white strip together to make a strip set. Press toward the black-and-white strip. Make four. Cut the strip sets into 2½"-wide segments. Cut 64 segments.

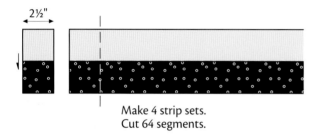

2½"

Make 4 strip sets.
Cut 64 segments.

2. Sew two segments from step 1 together as shown; press. Refer to "Four-Patch Units" on page 15 for guidance on positioning and pressing the center seam allowance. Make 32 units.

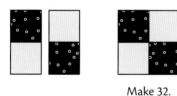

Make 32.

3. Sew one 2½" x 42" black-and-white strip and one 4½" x 42" red strip together to make a strip set. Press toward the red strip. Make two. Cut the strip sets into 2½"-wide segments. Cut 32 segments.

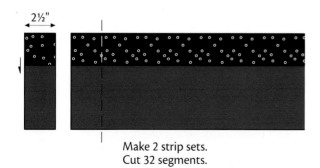

2½"

Make 2 strip sets.
Cut 32 segments.

4. Sew one unit from step 2, one segment from step 3, and one 2½" x 4½" red rectangle together as shown to make a corner unit; press. Make 32 units.

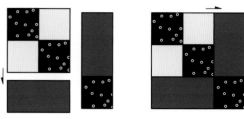

Make 32.

5. Sew one 2½" x 42" black-with-circles strip and one 4½" x 42" white strip together to make a strip set. Press toward the black strip. Make four. Cut the strip sets into 4½"-wide segments. Cut 32 segments.

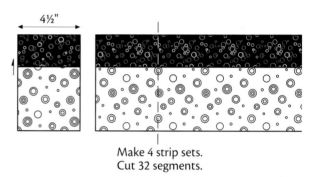

4½"

Make 4 strip sets.
Cut 32 segments.

6. Sew one segment from step 5 and one 2½" x 6½" black-with-circles rectangle together as shown to make a unit; press. Make 32 units.

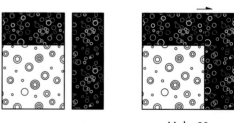

Make 32.

7. Sew two units from step 4 and two units from step 6 together as shown to make a block; press. Refer to "Four-Patch Units" on page 15 for guidance on positioning and pressing the center seam allowance. Make 16 blocks.

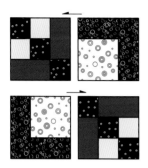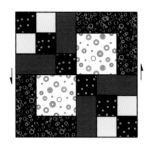

Make 16.

Assembling the Quilt Top

For detailed instructions, refer to "Quilts with Sashing Strips" on page 16.

1. Arrange five 2½" x 12½" striped rectangles and four blocks, rotating every other block 90° so that the four-patch units will form diagonal lines across the quilt as shown in the assembly diagram at right. Sew the sashing rectangles and blocks together; press. Make four rows.

Make 4.

2. Arrange and sew together three 2½" black-with-circles squares, two 2½" black-and-white squares, and four 2½" x 12½" striped rectangles as shown to make sashing row A; press. Make three rows.

Sashing row A.
Make 3.

3. Arrange and sew together three 2½" black-and-white squares, two 2½" black-with-circles squares, and four 2½" x 12½" striped rectangles as shown to make sashing row B; press. Make two rows.

Sashing row B.
Make 2.

4. Sew the block rows and sashing rows A and B together, alternating them as shown in the assembly diagram. Be sure the block rows are placed correctly so that the black-and-white squares form a chain across the quilt top. Press the seams toward the sashing rows.

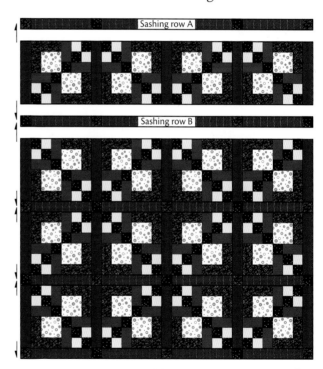

Assembly diagram

5. Refer to "Borders" on page 17. Measure, cut, and sew the 1¼"-wide yellow inner-border strips and then the 6¾"-wide black floral outer-border strips to the quilt top.

Finishing the Quilt

For detailed instructions on the following techniques, refer to "Finishing Your Quilt" on page 19.

1. Cut and piece the backing fabric so it is 4" to 6" larger than the quilt top. Layer the quilt top with batting and backing. Baste the layers together.

2. Hand or machine quilt as desired. You may wish to randomly quilt a medallion in various sizes over the blocks, sashing, and borders.

3. Square up the quilt sandwich.

4. Add a hanging sleeve, if desired.

5. Using the 2"-wide striped strips, sew the binding to the quilt. Add a label, if desired.

Stepping OUT

The perky polka-dot fabrics and big 16" blocks are certain to make this quilt especially fun. The eye-catching orange print and pleasing purple combine with a touch of yellow to produce a very playful quilt.

Finished Quilt Size: 73" x 91½"
Finished Block Size: 16"

Materials

Yardages are based on 42″-wide fabrics.

2⅔ yards of background floral print for blocks and sashing

2⅜ yards of yellow floral print for outer border

1¾ yards of orange print for blocks, sashing squares, and binding

1⅝ yards of purple-dot print for blocks and inner border

1⅓ yards of yellow-and-orange stripe for sashing

⅝ yard of yellow tonal print for blocks

6 yards of fabric for backing

78" x 97" piece of batting

Cutting

All measurements include ¼″-wide seam allowances. Cut all strips across the width of the fabric (selvage to selvage) unless instructed otherwise.

From the purple-dot print, cut:

18 strips, 2½" x 42"; crosscut into 288 squares, 2½" x 2½"

7 strips, 1" x 42"

From the yellow tonal print, cut:

3 strips, 5¼" x 42"; crosscut into 24 rectangles, 4½" x 5¼"

From the orange print, cut:

2 strips, 4½" x 42"; crosscut into 12 squares, 4½" x 4½"

2 strips, 3" x 42"; crosscut into 20 squares, 3" x 3"

9 strips, 2½" x 42"; crosscut into 144 squares, 2½" x 2½"

9 strips, 2" x 42"

From the background floral print, cut:

3 strips, 12½" x 42"; crosscut into 48 rectangles, 2½" x 12½"

3 strips, 8½" x 42"; crosscut into 48 rectangles, 2½" x 8½"

16 strips, 1½" x 42"

From the yellow-and-orange stripe, cut:

32 strips, 1¼" x 42"

From the *lengthwise grain* of the yellow floral print, cut:

4 strips, 7½" x 80"

Making the Blocks

1. Using the flying-geese-unit technique on page 14, draw a diagonal line from corner to corner on the wrong side of the 2½" purple-dot squares. Sew four purple-dot squares to each 4½" x 5¼" yellow rectangle as shown; press. Cut 48 flying-geese units. Set aside the remaining purple-dot squares for steps 3 and 5.

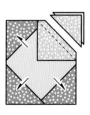 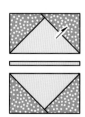

Make 48.

2. Sew four flying-geese units, four 2½" orange squares, and one 4½" orange square together as shown to make one center unit; press. Make 12 units.

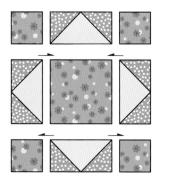 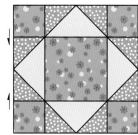

Make 12.

3. Using the square-and-rectangle-unit technique on page 12 and 96 of the marked squares from step 1, sew a purple-dot square to each end of an 8½" background floral rectangle as shown; press. Make 48 units.

Make 48.

4. Sew four units from step 3, four 2½" orange squares, and one center unit from step 2 together as shown; press. Make 12.

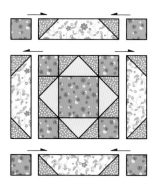 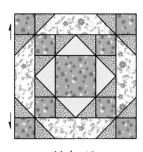

Make 12.

5. Using the square-and-rectangle-unit technique and the remaining marked squares from step 1, sew a purple-dot square to each end of a 12½" background floral rectangle as shown; press. Make 48 units.

Make 48.

6. Sew four units from step 5, four 2½" orange squares, and one unit from step 4 together as shown to make a block; press. Make 12 blocks.

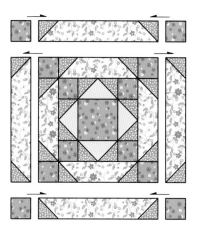

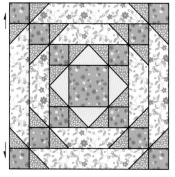

Make 12.

Assembling the Quilt Top

For detailed instructions, refer to "Quilts with Sashing Strips" on page 16.

1. Refer to "Making Strip Sets" on page 11. Sew one 1½" x 42" background floral strip between two 1¼" x 42" striped strips to make a strip set. Press toward the stripe. Make 16. Crosscut the strip sets into 16½"-wide segments. Cut 31 segments.

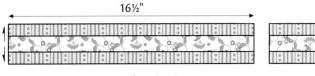

Make 16 strip sets.
Cut 31 segments.

2. Arrange and sew together four segments from step 1 and three blocks, alternating them as shown to make a block row; press. Make four rows.

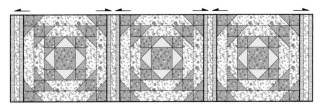

Make 4.

3. Arrange and sew together three segments from step 1 and four 3" orange squares as shown to make a sashing row; press. Make five rows.

Make 5.

4. Sew the block rows and sashing rows together, alternating them as shown in the assembly diagram. Press the seams toward the sashing rows.

Assembly diagram

5. Refer to "Borders" on page 17. Measure, cut, and sew the 1"-wide purple-dot inner-border strips and then the 7½"-wide yellow floral outer-border strips to the quilt top.

Finishing the Quilt

For detailed instructions on the following techniques, refer to "Finishing Your Quilt" on page 19.

1. Cut and piece the backing fabric so it is 4" to 6" larger than the quilt top. Layer the quilt top with batting and backing. Baste the layers together.

2. Hand or machine quilt as desired. You may wish to quilt a continuous design over the center of the quilt. Quilt small loops in the inner border and a continuous design of leaves and loops in the outer border.

3. Square up the quilt sandwich.

4. Add a hanging sleeve, if desired.

5. Using the 2"-wide orange strips, sew the binding to the quilt. Add a label, if desired.

Garden STARS

The addition of plain sashing provides the perfect showcase for the Star blocks in this charming quilt. Using two fabrics for the sashing corners creates continuous chains of squares that appear to weave through the stars, making this ordinary quilt a real winner.

Finished Quilt Size: 73½" x 87½"
Finished Block Size: 12"

Materials

Yardages are based on 42˝-wide fabrics.

2⅞ yards of cream print for blocks and sashing
2¼ yards of sunflower print for outer border
1⅝ yards of navy print for blocks and binding
¾ yard of red print for blocks and sashing squares
¾ yard of gold print for blocks and sashing squares
¾ yard of blue tonal print for blocks
⅓ yard of yellowish orange tonal fabric for inner border
5⅞ yards of fabric for backing
79" x 93" piece of batting

Cutting

All measurements include ¼˝-wide seam allowances.
Cut all strips across the width of the fabric (selvage to selvage) unless instructed otherwise.

From the cream print, cut:
20 strips, 2½" x 42"; crosscut *10 strips* into 160 squares, 2½" x 2½"
17 strips, 2½" x 42"; crosscut into 49 rectangles, 2½" x 12½"

From the red print, cut:
9 strips, 2½" x 42"; crosscut *4 strips* into 55 squares, 2½" x 2½"

From the gold print, cut:
9 strips, 2½" x 42"; crosscut *4 strips* into 55 squares, 2½" x 2½"

From the blue tonal print, cut:
5 strips, 4½" x 42"; crosscut into 80 rectangles, 2½" x 4½"

From the navy print, cut:
5 strips, 6½" x 42"; crosscut into 80 rectangles, 2½" x 6½"
9 strips, 2" x 42"

From the yellowish orange tonal fabric, cut:
7 strips, 1¼" x 42"

From the *lengthwise grain* of the sunflower print, cut:
4 strips, 7½" x 76"

Making the Blocks

1. Refer to "Making Strip Sets" on page 11. Sew one 2½" x 42" cream strip and one 2½" x 42" red strip together to make a strip set. Press toward the red strip. Make five. Cut the strip sets into 2½"-wide segments. Cut 80 segments.

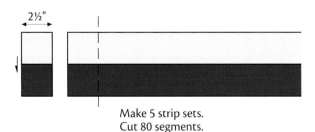

2½"

Make 5 strip sets.
Cut 80 segments.

2. Sew two segments from step 1 together as shown; press. Refer to "Four-Patch Units" on page 15 for guidance on positioning and pressing the center seam allowance. Make 40 units.

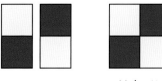

Make 40.

3. Sew one 2½" x 42" cream strip and one 2½" x 42" gold strip together to make a strip set. Press toward the gold strip. Make five. Cut the strip sets into 2½"-wide segments. Cut 80 segments.

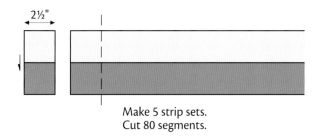

2½"

Make 5 strip sets.
Cut 80 segments.

4. Sew two segments from step 3 together as shown; press. Again refer to "Four-Patch Units" for guidance on positioning and pressing the center seam allowance. Make 40 units.

Make 40.

5. Using the square-and-rectangle-unit technique on page 12, draw a diagonal line from corner to corner on the wrong side of the 2½" cream squares. Sew a cream square on one end of a blue rectangle as shown; press. Make 80 units. You'll have 80 cream squares left over and will use them in the next two steps.

Make 80.

6. Using the square-and-rectangle-unit technique, draw a diagonal line from corner to corner on the wrong side of the 2½" red squares. Sew a red square and a cream square from step 5 on opposite ends of a navy rectangle as shown; press. Make 40 units.

Make 40.

7. Using the square-and-rectangle-unit technique, draw a diagonal line from corner to corner on the wrong side of the 2½" gold squares. Sew a gold square and a cream square from step 5 on opposite ends of a navy rectangle as shown; press. Make 40 units.

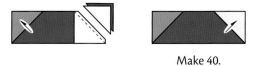

Make 40.

8. Sew one unit from step 2, one unit from step 5, and one unit from step 6 together as shown to make a red unit; press. Make 40 units.

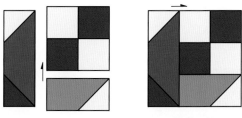

Make 40.

9. Sew one unit from step 4, one unit from step 5, and one unit from step 7 together as shown to make one gold unit; press. Make 40 units.

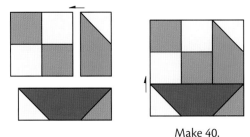

Make 40.

10. Sew two red units and two gold units together as shown to make a block; press. For guidance on positioning and pressing the center seam allowance, refer to "Four-Patch Units." Make 20 blocks.

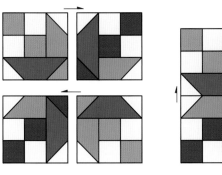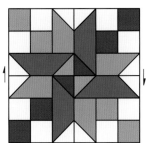

Make 20.

Assembling the Quilt Top

For detailed instructions, refer to "Quilts with Sashing Strips" on page 16.

1. Arrange five 2½" x 12½" cream rectangles and four blocks, rotating every other block 90° so that the four-patch units will form diagonal lines across the quilt as shown in the assembly diagram at right. Sew the sashing strips and blocks together; press. Make five rows.

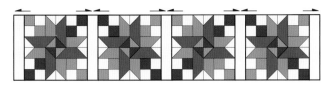

Make 5.

2. Arrange and sew together three 2½" gold squares, two 2½" red squares, and four 2½" x 12½" cream rectangles as shown to make sashing row A; press. Make three rows.

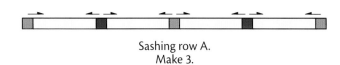

Sashing row A.
Make 3.

3. Arrange and sew together three 2½" red squares, two 2½" gold squares, and four 2½" x 12½" cream rectangles as shown to make sashing row B; press. Make three rows.

Sashing row B.
Make 3.

4. Sew the block rows and sashing rows A and B together, alternating them as shown in the assembly diagram. Be sure the block rows are placed correctly so that the red-and-gold squares form chains across the quilt top. Press the seams toward the sashing rows.

Assembly diagram

5. Refer to "Borders" on page 17. Measure, cut, and sew the 1¼"-wide yellowish orange inner-border strips and then the 7½"-wide sunflower print outer-border strips to the quilt top.

Finishing the Quilt

For detailed instructions on the following techniques, refer to "Finishing Your Quilt" on page 19.

1. Cut and piece the backing fabric so it is 4" to 6" larger than the quilt top. Layer the quilt top with batting and backing. Baste the layers together.

2. Hand or machine quilt as desired. You may wish to quilt a medallion in the center of the blocks and a continuous leaf design over the sashing. Quilt a continuous design in the outer border.

3. Square up the quilt sandwich.

4. Add a hanging sleeve, if desired.

5. Using the 2"-wide navy strips, sew the binding to the quilt. Add a label, if desired.

O Christmas TREE

This delightful quilt will really put you in the holiday spirit. Use machine embroidery to embellish your trees with ornaments or presents. Whether you use it to celebrate the Twelve Days of Christmas or as an Advent calendar, you'll want to include this quilt in your Christmas decorating.

Finished Quilt Size: 48" x 51½"
Finished Block Size: 8"

Materials

Yardages are based on 42˝-wide fabrics. Fat quarters measure 18˝ x 21˝.

1⅔ yards of green Christmas lights print for outer border and binding
1 fat quarter *each* of 6 assorted green prints for blocks
1¼ yards of cream print for blocks and sashing
½ yard of red tonal print for sashing and inner border
⅛ yard of brown plaid for blocks
3¼ yards of fabric for backing
53" x 57" piece of batting
72 to 96 fusible rhinestones (optional)

Cutting

All measurements include ¼"-wide seam allowances. Cut all strips across the width of the fabric (selvage to selvage) unless instructed otherwise.

From the brown plaid, cut:
1 rectangle, 2" x 24"

From the cream print, cut:
2 strips, 4½" x 42"; crosscut into 24 rectangles, 2½" x 4½"
2 strips, 3¾" x 24"
3 strips, 3¼" x 42"; crosscut into 24 rectangles, 3¼" x 3¾"

2 strips, 2½" x 42"; crosscut into 24 squares, 2½" x 2½"
4 strips, 2" x 42"; crosscut into 15 rectangles, 2" x 8½"

From *each* of the 6 assorted green fat quarters, cut:
2 rectangles, 3¼" x 7½" (12 total)
2 rectangles, 2½" x 8½" (12 total)
2 rectangles, 2½" x 4½" (12 total)

From the red tonal print, cut:
8 strips, 1½" x 42"

From the *lengthwise grain* of the green Christmas lights print, cut:
4 strips, 5½" x 51"
2 strips, 4½" x 42"
4 strips, 2" x 53"

Making the Blocks

1. Refer to "Making Strip Sets" on page 11. Sew one 2" x 24" brown plaid strip between two 3¾" x 24" cream strips to make a strip set. Press toward the brown strip. Cut the strip set into 1¾"-wide segments. Cut 12 segments.

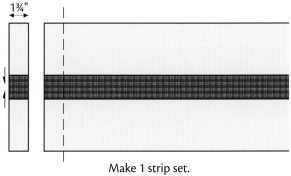

Make 1 strip set.
Cut 12 segments.

2. Using the square-and-rectangle-unit technique on page 12, draw a diagonal line from corner to corner on the wrong side of the 2½" cream squares. Sew two cream squares on opposite ends of a 2½" x 8½" green rectangle as shown; press. Make 12 units.

Make 12.

3. Using the rectangle-to-rectangle-unit technique on page 13, draw a diagonal line on the wrong side of the 3¼" x 3¾" cream rectangles. Sew two cream rectangles on opposite ends of a 3¼" x 7½" green rectangle as shown; press. Make 12 units.

Make 12.

4. Using the rectangle-to-rectangle-unit technique, draw a diagonal line on the wrong side of the 2½" x 4½" cream rectangles. Sew two cream rectangles on opposite ends of a 2½" x 4½" green rectangle as shown; press. Make 12 units.

Make 12.

5. Each Tree block is made from one green fabric. Sew one segment from step 1, one unit from step 2, one matching unit from step 3, and one matching unit from step 4 together as shown to make a block; press. Make 12 blocks.

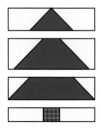

Make 12.

Assembling the Quilt Top

1. Assemble and sew four Tree blocks and five 2" x 8½" cream rectangles into a vertical row as shown; press. Make three vertical rows.

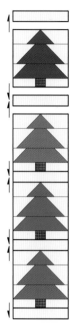

Make 3.

2. Refer to "Making Strip Sets" on page 11. Sew one 4½" x 42" strip of Christmas lights print between two 1½" x 42" red strips to make a strip set; press. Make two. Measure the length of each of the three vertical rows. If they differ, calculate the average and consider this the length. Cut each strip set to fit that measurement.

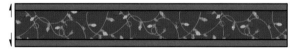

Make 2.

3. Sew the rows of Tree blocks and the two trimmed strip sets from step 2 together as shown; press.

4. Refer to "Borders" on page 17. Measure, cut, and sew the 1½"-wide red inner-border strips and then the 5½"-wide outer-border strips of Christmas lights print to the quilt top.

Finishing the Quilt

For detailed instructions on the following techniques, refer to "Finishing Your Quilt" on page 19.

1. Cut and piece the backing fabric so it is 4" to 6" larger than the quilt top. Layer the quilt top with batting and backing. Baste the layers together.

2. Hand or machine quilt as desired. You may wish to quilt a medallion in the center of the trees and a meandering design in the background. Quilt a small zigzag design over the red sashing and a continuous design of loops and swirls in the green sashing and outer border. I embellished each of my trees randomly with six to eight fusible rhinestones.

3. Square up the quilt sandwich.

4. Add a hanging sleeve, if desired.

5. Using the 2"-wide strips of Christmas lights print, sew the binding to the quilt. Add a label, if desired.

Flower CHAIN

Big 16" blocks combined with pieced sashing make this bed-sized quilt a breeze to stitch together. The softly blended colors have a romantic look, so you're sure to feel right at home with this lovely quilt.

Finished Quilt Size: 90" x 108"
Finished Block Size: 16"

Materials

Yardages are based on 42˝-wide fabrics.

3½ yards of white tonal print for blocks
3¼ yards of large-scale green floral print for outer
    border
1⅜ yards of dark pink floral print for blocks
1⅓ yards of green tonal print for blocks and sashing
    squares
1⅓ yards of pink-and-yellow stripe for sashing
⅞ yard of light pink floral print for blocks
⅝ yard of yellow tonal print for sashing
½ yard of small-scale green floral print for blocks
¾ yard of dark pink tonal print for binding
8½ yards of fabric for backing
95" x 113" piece of batting

Cutting

All measurements include ¼˝-wide seam allowances. Cut all strips across the width of the fabric (selvage to selvage) unless instructed otherwise.

From the white tonal print, cut:
5 strips, 12½" x 42"; crosscut into 80 rectangles,
    2½" x 12½"
20 strips, 2½" x 42"; crosscut *10 strips* into 160
    squares, 2½" x 2½"

From the green tonal print, cut:
17 strips, 2½" x 42"; crosscut 7 *strips* into 110 squares,
    2½" x 2½"

From the dark pink floral print, cut:
10 strips, 4½" x 42"; crosscut into 80 squares,
    4½" x 4½"

From the small-scale green floral print, cut:
3 strips, 4½" x 42"; crosscut into 20 squares,
    4½" x 4½"

From the light pink floral print, cut:
10 strips, 2½" x 42"; crosscut into 160 squares,
    2½" x 2½"

From the pink-and-yellow stripe, cut:
17 strips, 2½" x 42"; crosscut into 49 rectangles,
    2½" x 12½"

From the yellow tonal print, cut:
7 strips, 2½" x 42"; crosscut into 98 squares,
    2½" x 2½"

From the *lengthwise grain* of the large-scale green floral print, cut:
4 strips, 8½" x 111"

From the dark pink tonal print, cut:
11 strips, 2" x 42"

Making the Blocks

1. Refer to "Making Strip Sets" on page 11. Sew one 2½" x 42" white strip and one 2½" x 42" green strip together to make a strip set. Press toward the green strip. Make 10. Cut the strip sets into 2½"-wide segments. Cut 160 segments.

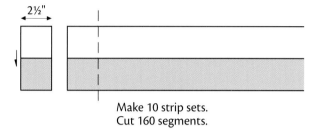

Make 10 strip sets.
Cut 160 segments.

2. Sew two segments from step 1 together as shown; press. Refer to "Four-Patch Units" on page 15 for guidance on positioning and pressing the center seam allowance. Make 80 units.

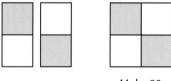

Make 80.

3. Using the square-on-square-unit technique on page 12, draw a diagonal line from corner to corner on the wrong side of the 2½" white squares. Sew a white square to adjacent corners of a dark pink floral square as shown; press. Make 80 units.

Make 80.

4. Sew four units from step 2, four units from step 3, and one 4½" small-scale green floral square together as shown; press. Make 20 units.

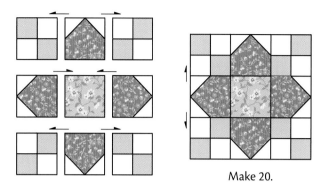

Make 20.

5. Using the square-and-rectangle-unit technique on page 12, draw a diagonal line from corner to corner on the wrong side of the 2½" light pink squares. Sew a light pink square to each end of a 12½" white rectangle as shown; press. Make 80 units.

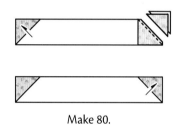

Make 80.

6. Sew one unit from step 4, four units from step 5, and four 2½" green squares together as shown to make a block; press. Make 20 blocks.

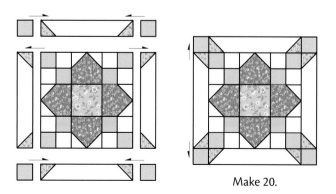

Make 20.

Assembling the Quilt Top

For detailed instructions, refer to "Quilts with Sashing Strips" on page 16.

1. Sew one 2½" x 12½" striped rectangle between two 2½" yellow squares to make a sashing unit. Refer to "Timely Tips" at right for guidance on pressing the seam allowances. Make 49.

Make 49.

2. Arrange and sew together five sashing units from step 1 and four blocks, alternating them as shown to make a block row; press. Make five rows.

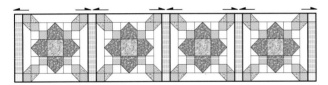

Make 5.

3. Arrange and sew together four sashing units from step 1 and five 2½" green squares as shown to make a sashing row; press. Make six rows.

Make 6.

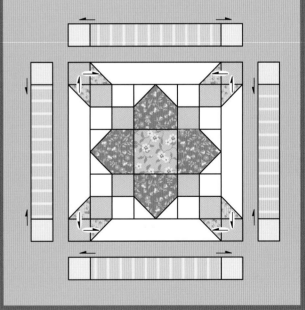

4. Sew the block rows and sashing rows together, alternating them as shown in the assembly diagram. Press the seams toward the sashing rows.

Assembly diagram

5. Refer to "Borders" on page 17. Measure, cut, and sew the 8½"-wide floral outer-border strips to the quilt top.

Finishing the Quilt

For detailed instructions on the following techniques, refer to "Finishing Your Quilt" on page 19.

1. Cut and piece the backing fabric so it is 4" to 6" larger than the quilt top. Layer the quilt top with batting and backing. Baste the layers together.

2. Hand or machine quilt as desired. You may wish to quilt a medallion in the center of the blocks and a meandering design in the background. Quilt a small loop design over the sashing and straight lines over the nine-patch units. Quilt a continuous design of large and small loops in the outer border.

3. Square up the quilt sandwich.

4. Add a hanging sleeve, if desired.

5. Using the 2"-wide dark pink strips, sew the binding to the quilt. Add a label, if desired.

Pinwheel PARTY

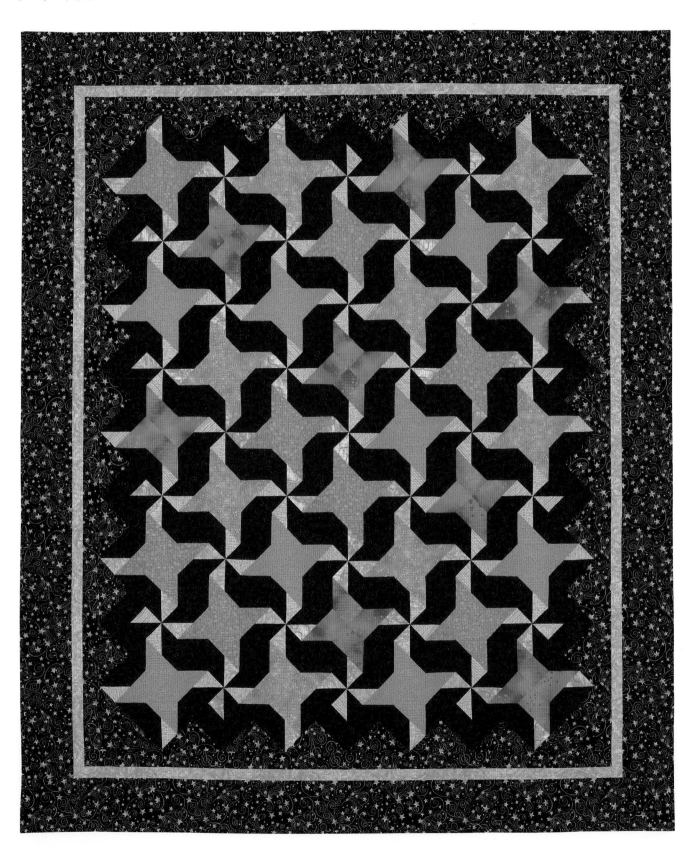

Simple squares and rectangles combine for a complex-looking quilt that's actually quite easy to make. The background for this quilt can be either light or dark. Choose different values of the same fabric color to add contrast and subtlety to the design.

Finished Quilt Size: 59¼" x 70½"
Finished Block Size: 8"

Materials

Yardages are based on 42"-wide fabrics.

2½ yards of black-and-orange star print for setting triangles, inner and outer borders, and binding

2 yards of black tonal print for blocks

⅓ yard *each* of 4 assorted orange tonal prints for blocks

¼ yard *each* of 3 assorted yellow tonal prints for blocks

⅝ yard of yellow-with-orange dots print for blocks and middle border

4 yards of fabric for backing

64" x 75" piece of batting

Cutting

All measurements include ¼"-wide seam allowances. Cut all strips across the width of the fabric (selvage to selvage) unless instructed otherwise.

From the black tonal print, cut:

10 strips, 4½" x 42"; crosscut into 156 rectangles, 2½" x 4½"

8 strips, 2½" x 42"; crosscut into 128 squares, 2½" x 2½"

From *each* of the 4 assorted orange tonal prints, cut:

2 strips (8 total), 4½" x 42"; crosscut into 128 rectangles, 2½" x 4½"

From *each* of the 3 assorted yellow tonal prints, cut:

3 strips (9 total), 2½" x 42"; crosscut into 107 squares, 2½" x 2½"

From the yellow-with-orange dots print, cut:

3 strips, 2½" x 42"; crosscut into 35 squares, 2½" x 2½"

6 strips, 1½" x 42"

From the *lengthwise grain* of the black-and-orange star print, cut:

4 strips, 5" x 65"

8 strips, 2" x 65"

From the remaining star print, cut:

7 squares, 7" x 7"; cut twice diagonally to yield 28 side triangles

2 squares, 7" x 7"; cut once diagonally to yield 4 corner triangles

Making the Blocks

1. Using the square-and-rectangle-unit technique on page 12, draw a diagonal line from corner to corner on the wrong side of the 2½" black squares. Sew a black square to one end of an orange rectangle as shown; press. Make 128 units.

Make 128.

2. Using the square-and-rectangle-unit technique, draw a diagonal line from corner to corner on the wrong side of the 2½" yellow and 2½" yellow-with-orange dots squares. Sew one square to one end of a black rectangle as shown; press. Make 142 units.

Make 142.

3. Arrange one unit from step 1 and one unit from step 2 in matching sets of four. You should have 32 sets. Set the remaining 14 units from step 2 aside for step 1 of "Assembling the Quilt Top." Sew the units together as shown to make a corner unit; press. Make 128 units.

Make 128.

4. Sew four matching corner units together, rotating the units 90° as shown to make a block; press. Refer to "Four-Patch Units" on page 15 for guidance on positioning and pressing the center seam allowance. Make 32 Pinwheel blocks.

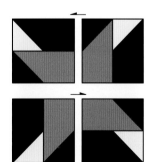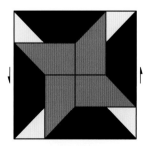

Make 32.

Assembling the Quilt Top

For detailed instructions, refer to "Quilts Set Diagonally" on page 17. The setting triangles have been cut slightly oversized. You will trim them after the quilt center is assembled.

1. Sew one unit from step 2 of "Making the Blocks" and one 2½" x 4½" black rectangle together as shown to make a setting unit; press. Make 14 units.

Make 14.

2. Sew two star print quarter-square triangles and one setting unit from step 1 together as shown to make a setting triangle; press. Make 14 setting triangles.

Make 14.

3. Arrange the blocks in diagonal rows as shown in the assembly diagram on page 55. Add the side setting triangles from step 2.

4. Sew the blocks and side setting triangles together into rows; press.

5. Sew the rows together, adding the star print half-square triangles last. Press the seams toward the star print triangles.

Assembly diagram

6. To trim and straighten the quilt top, align the ¼" mark on your ruler with the outermost points of the blocks. Use a rotary cutter to trim any excess fabric, leaving a ¼"-wide seam allowance. Square the corners of the quilt top as necessary.

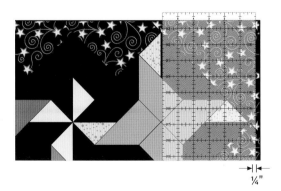

¼"

7. Refer to "Borders" on page 17. Measure, cut, and sew four of the 2"-wide star print inner-border strips, then the 1½"-wide yellow-with-orange dots middle-border strips, and lastly the 5"-wide star print outer-border strips to the quilt top.

Finishing the Quilt

For detailed instructions on the following techniques, refer to "Finishing Your Quilt" on page 19.

1. Cut and piece the backing fabric so it is 4" to 6" larger than the quilt top. Layer the quilt top with batting and backing. Baste the layers together.

2. Hand or machine quilt as desired. You may wish to quilt a medallion in the center of the blocks and a small continuous star-and-loops design over the black background, side and corner setting triangles, and inner border. Quilt a continuous loop in the middle border and a larger continuous star-and-loops design in the outer border.

3. Square up the quilt sandwich.

4. Add a hanging sleeve, if desired.

5. Using the remaining 2"-wide star print strips, sew the binding to the quilt. Add a label, if desired.

Pansy PARADE

This wonderful bed-sized quilt is simplicity itself! The combination of the pieced blocks and sashing mimic the look of spring flowers. Capture the essence of spring throughout the year with this quick quilt.

Finished Quilt Size: 72" x 86"
Finished Block Size: 12"

Materials

Yardages are based on 42"-wide fabrics.

2¼ yards of large-scale floral print for outer border and binding
1⅛ yards of dark purple tonal print for blocks
1 yard of medium green tonal print for sashing
⅞ yard of light green tonal print for sashing
⅞ yard of light purple tonal print for blocks
⅞ yard of cream background print for blocks
½ yard of light floral print for blocks
½ yard of yellow tonal print for blocks
¼ yard of dark green tonal print for sashing
5⅝ yards of fabric for backing
77" x 91" piece of batting

Cutting

All measurements include ¼"-wide seam allowances. Cut all strips across the width of the fabric (selvage to selvage) unless instructed otherwise.

From the yellow tonal print, cut:
5 strips, 2½" x 42"

From the dark purple print, cut:
5 strips, 4½" x 42"; crosscut into 80 rectangles,
    2½" x 4½"
5 strips, 2½" x 42"

From the cream background print, cut:
10 strips, 2½" x 42"

From the light purple tonal print, cut:
10 strips, 2½" x 42"

From the light floral print, cut:
3 strips, 4½" x 42"; crosscut into 20 squares,
    4½" x 4½"

From the light green tonal print, cut:
4 strips, 6½" x 42"

From the medium green tonal print, cut:
8 strips, 3½" x 42"

From the dark green tonal print, cut:
2 strips, 2½" x 42"; crosscut into 30 squares,
    2½" x 2½"

From the *lengthwise grain* of the large-scale floral print, cut:
4 strips, 7½" x 75"
5 strips, 2" x 66"

Making the Blocks

Refer to "Making Strip Sets" on page 11.

1. Sew one 2½" x 42" yellow strip and one 2½" x 42" dark purple strip together to make a strip set. Press toward the purple strip. Make five. Cut the strip sets into 2½"-wide segments. Cut 80 segments.

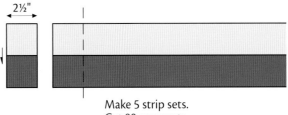

Make 5 strip sets.
Cut 80 segments.

2. Sew one segment from step 1 and one 2½" x 4½" dark purple rectangle together as shown to make a corner unit; press. Make 80 units.

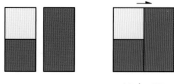

Make 80.

3. Sew one 2½" x 42" cream strip and one 2½" x 42" light purple strip together to make a strip set. Press toward the purple strip. Make 10. Cut the strip sets into 4½"-wide segments. Cut 80 segments.

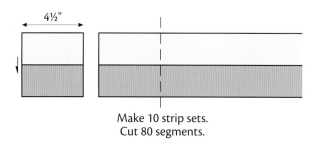

Make 10 strip sets.
Cut 80 segments.

4. Sew four units from step 2, four segments from step 3, and one 4½" light floral square together as shown to make a block; press. Make 20 blocks.

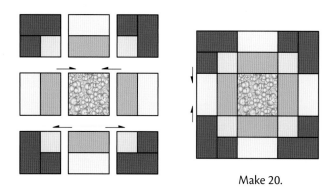

Make 20.

Assembling the Quilt Top

For detailed instructions, refer to "Quilts with Sashing Strips" on page 16.

1. Refer to "Making Strip Sets" on page 11. Sew one 6½" x 42" light green strip between two 3½" x 42" medium green strips to make a strip set. Press toward the medium green strips. Make four. Cut the strip sets into 2½"-wide segments. Cut 49 segments.

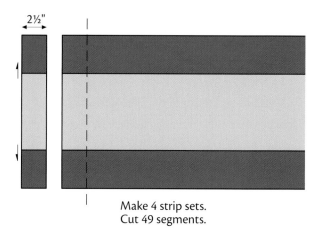

Make 4 strip sets.
Cut 49 segments.

2. Arrange and sew together five segments from step 1 and four blocks, alternating them as shown to make a block row; press. Make five rows.

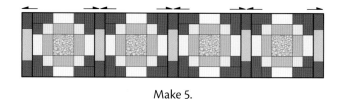

Make 5.

3. Arrange and sew together four segments from step 1 and five 2½" dark green squares as shown to make a sashing row; press. Make six rows.

Make 6.

4. Sew the block rows and sashing rows together, alternating them as shown in the assembly diagram. Press the seams toward the sashing rows.

Assembly diagram

5. Refer to "Borders" on page 17. Measure, cut, and sew the 7½"-wide large-scale floral outer-border strips to the quilt top.

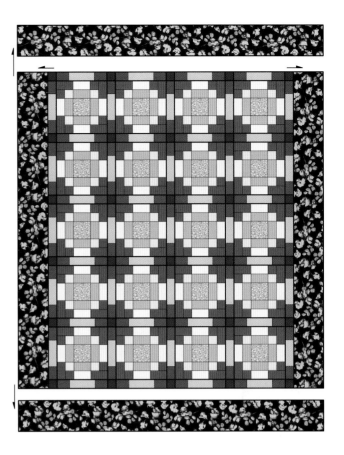

Finishing the Quilt

For detailed instructions on the following techniques, refer to "Finishing Your Quilt" on page 19.

1. Cut and piece the backing fabric so it is 4" to 6" larger than the quilt top. Layer the quilt top with batting and backing. Baste the layers together.

2. Hand or machine quilt as desired. You may wish to quilt a continuous design over the center of the quilt and straight lines in the outer border.

3. Square up the quilt sandwich.

4. Add a hanging sleeve, if desired.

5. Using the 2"-wide large-scale floral strips, sew the binding to the quilt. Add a label, if desired.

Window BOXES

The graphic, contemporary design and warm, earthy colors make this terrific quilt very pleasing to behold. The light print sparkles against the darker prints, while the narrow gray sashing seems to float in front of the blocks as though you're looking through a window.

Finished Quilt Size: 64¾" x 64¾"
Finished Block Size: 12"

Materials

Yardages are based on 42˝-wide fabrics.

2 yards of gray fern batik for outer border
1⅛ yards of gray tonal batik for sashing, inner
    border, and binding
⅞ yard of yellowish tan batik for blocks
¾ yard of rust batik for blocks
⅔ yard of brown batik for blocks
⅝ yard of cream batik for blocks
4⅜ yards of fabric for backing
70" x 70" piece of batting

Cutting

All measurements include ¼˝-wide seam allowances.
Cut all strips across the width of the fabric (selvage to selvage) unless instructed otherwise.

From the rust batik, cut:
4 strips, 4½" x 42"
2 strips, 2½" x 42"

From the yellowish tan batik, cut:
10 strips, 2½" x 42"

From the brown batik, cut:
8 strips, 2½" x 42"

From the cream batik, cut:
4 strips, 4½" x 42"

From the gray tonal batik, cut:
7 strips, 2" x 42"
6 strips, 1¾" x 42"
8 strips, 1¼" x 42"; crosscut *4 strips* into 12
    rectangles, 1¼" x 12½"

From the *lengthwise grain* of the gray fern batik, cut:
4 strips, 6½" x 68"

Making the Blocks

Refer to "Making Strip Sets" on page 11.

1. Sew one 2½" x 42" rust strip and one 2½" x 42" yellowish tan strip together to make a strip set. Press toward the rust strip. Make two. Cut the strip sets into 2½"-wide segments. Cut 32 segments.

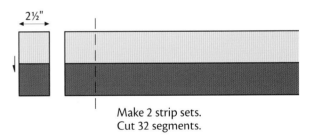

Make 2 strip sets.
Cut 32 segments.

2. Sew two segments from step 1 together as shown to make a four-patch unit. Press the seams as shown. Make 16 units.

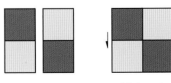

Make 16.

3. Sew one 2½" x 42" brown strip and one 2½" x 42" yellowish tan strip together to make a strip set. Make four. Press two strip sets toward the brown and label these strip set A. Press the other two strip sets toward the yellowish tan and label these strip set B. Cut the strip sets into 4½"-wide segments. Cut a total of 32 segments.

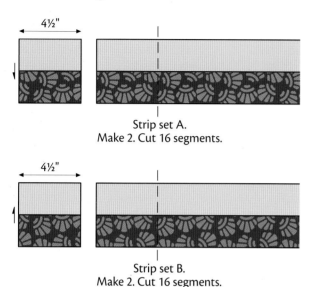

Strip set A.
Make 2. Cut 16 segments.

Strip set B.
Make 2. Cut 16 segments.

4. Arrange one four-patch unit from step 2 between one A segment and one B segment, positioning the pressed seams in the directions indicated. Sew the units together to make a center unit; press. Make 16 units.

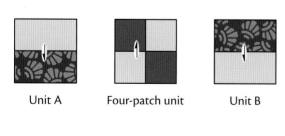

Unit A   Four-patch unit   Unit B

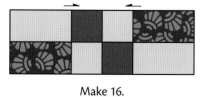

Make 16.

5. Sew one 2½" x 42" brown strip, one 2½" x 42" yellowish tan strip, one 4½" x 42" rust strip, and one 4½" x 42" cream strip together as shown to make a strip set. Press the seams as shown. Make four. Cut the strip sets into 4½"-wide segments. Cut 32 segments.

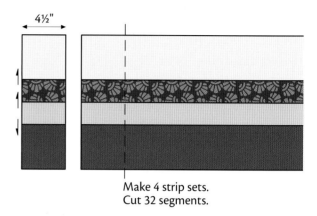

Make 4 strip sets.
Cut 32 segments.

6. Sew one center unit from step 4 between two segments from step 5 as shown to make a block; press. Make 16 blocks.

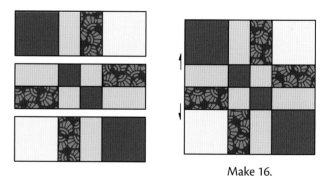

Make 16.

Assembling the Quilt Top

For detailed instructions, refer to "Quilts with Sashing Strips" on page 16.

1. Arrange and sew three 1¼" x 12½" gray sashing strips and four blocks, alternating them

and rotating the blocks 90° as shown to make a block row; press. Make four rows.

Make 4.

2. Measure the length of each of the four block rows. If they differ, calculate the average and consider this the length. Sew the 1¼" x 42" gray strips together end to end to make a continuous strip. From this long strip, cut three sashing strips the length of your row measurement.

3. Sew the block rows and the three sashing strips from step 2 together, alternating them as shown in the assembly diagram. Press the seams toward the sashing strips.

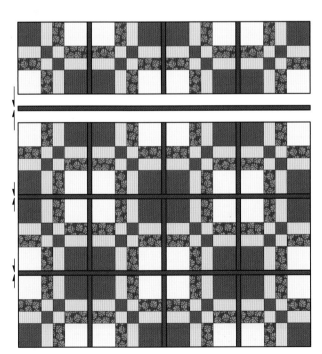

Assembly diagram

4. Refer to "Borders" on page 17. Measure, cut, and sew the 1¾"-wide gray inner-border strips and the 6½"-wide fern batik outer-border strips to the quilt top.

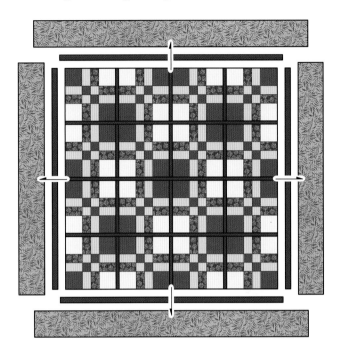

Finishing the Quilt

For detailed instructions on the following techniques, refer to "Finishing Your Quilt" on page 19.

1. Cut and piece the backing fabric so it is 4" to 6" larger than the quilt top. Layer the quilt top with batting and backing. Baste the layers together.

2. Hand or machine quilt as desired. You may wish to randomly quilt a circle-and-spiral design in various sizes over the entire surface of the quilt top.

3. Square up the quilt sandwich.

4. Add a hanging sleeve, if desired.

5. Using the 2"-wide gray tonal strips, sew the binding to the quilt. Add a label, if desired.

Spinning STARS

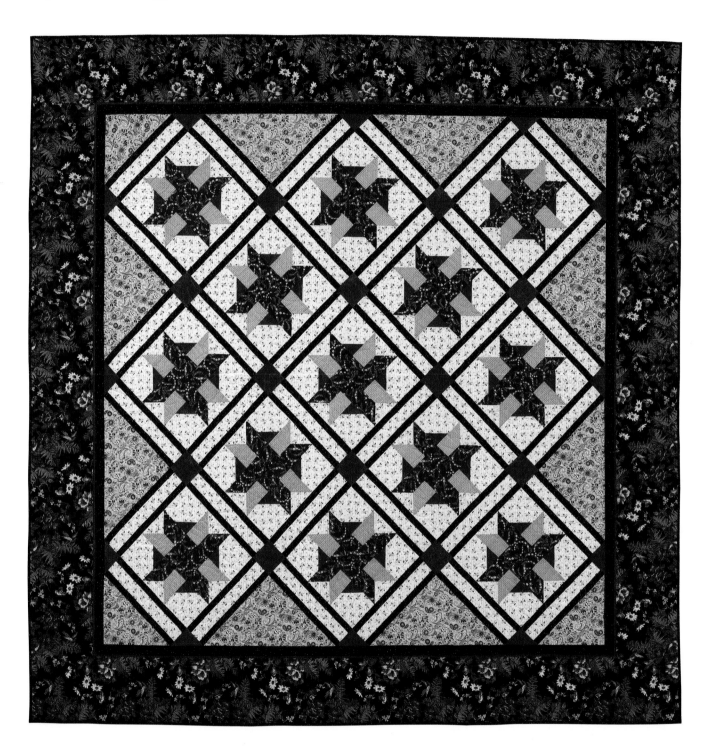

I love the energetic design of this Star block. I used two blue fabrics to give the blocks added dimension, and I tucked extra red pieces into the corners to further enhance the effect. The narrow dark sashing gives this stunning quilt a look of sophistication, while it also makes the sewing easier. We're always in favor of that!

Finished Quilt Size: 82⅝" x 82⅝"
Finished Block Size: 12"

Materials

Yardages are based on 42″-wide fabrics.

2⅝ yards of large-scale floral for outer border
2¼ yards of cream background print for blocks and sashing
2 yards of navy tonal print for sashing, inner border, and binding
1 yard of red tonal print for blocks, sashing squares, and flat piping
1 yard of paisley print for setting triangles
⅞ yard of small-scale navy floral for blocks
⅝ yard of light blue tonal print for blocks
8 yards of fabric for backing
88" x 88" piece of batting

Cutting

All measurements include ¼″-wide seam allowances. Cut all strips across the width of the fabric (selvage to selvage) unless instructed otherwise.

From the red tonal print, cut:

2 strips, 3½" x 42"; crosscut into 12 squares, 3½" x 3½"
4 strips, 2½" x 42"; crosscut into 52 squares, 2½" x 2½"
7 strips, 1" x 42"
3 squares, 5¾" x 5¾"; cut twice diagonally to yield 12 triangles

From the cream background print, cut:

7 strips, 4½" x 42"; crosscut into 52 squares, 4½" x 4½"
7 strips, 2½" x 42"; crosscut into 104 squares, 2½" x 2½"
12 strips, 2" x 42"

From the light blue tonal print, cut:

4 strips, 4½" x 42"; crosscut into 52 rectangles, 2½" x 4½"

From the small-scale navy floral, cut:

4 strips, 6½" x 42"; crosscut into 52 rectangles, 2½" x 6½"

From the navy tonal print, cut:

16 strips, 2" x 42"
24 strips, 1¼" x 42"

From the paisley print, cut:

2 squares, 18½" x 18½"; cut twice diagonally to yield 8 side triangles
2 squares, 9½" x 9½"; cut once diagonally to yield 4 corner triangles

From the *lengthwise grain* of the large-scale floral print, cut:

4 strips, 8½" x 86"

Making the Blocks

1. Using the square-on-square-unit technique on page 12, draw a diagonal line from corner to corner on the wrong side of the 2½" red squares. Sew one red square to one 4½" cream square as shown; press. Make 52 units.

Make 52.

2. Using the square-and-rectangle-unit technique on page 12, draw a diagonal line from corner to corner on the wrong side of the 2½" cream squares. Sew one cream square to one end of a 2½" x 4½" light blue rectangle as shown; press. Make 52 units. You'll have 52 cream squares left over to use in the next step.

Make 52.

3. Sew one cream square from step 2 to one end of a 2½" x 6½" navy floral rectangle as shown; press. Make 52 units.

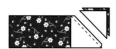

Make 52.

4. Sew one unit from step 1 and one unit from step 2 together as shown; press. Make 52.

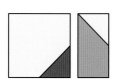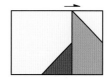

Make 52.

5. Sew one unit from step 3 and one unit from step 4 together as shown to make a unit; press. Make 52 units.

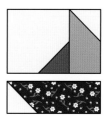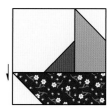

Make 52.

6. Sew four units from step 5 together, rotating the units 90° as shown to make a block; press. Refer to "Four-Patch Units" on page 15 for guidance on positioning and pressing the center seam allowance. Make 13 blocks.

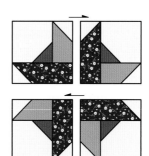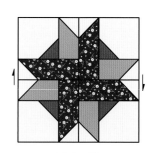

Make 13.

Assembling the Quilt Top

For detailed instructions, refer to "Quilts Set Diagonally" on page 17. The setting triangles have been cut slightly oversized. You will trim them after the quilt center is assembled.

1. Refer to "Making Strip Sets" on page 11. Sew one 2" x 42" cream strip between two 1¼" x 42" navy tonal strips to make a strip set. Press toward the navy strips. Make 12. Cut the strip sets into 12½"-wide segments. Cut 36 segments.

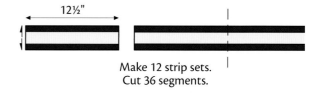

12½"

Make 12 strip sets.
Cut 36 segments.

2. Arrange the blocks, the sashing units from step 1, the 3½" red sashing squares, the 5¾" red sashing triangles, and the paisley side and corner triangles in diagonal rows as shown in the assembly diagram below.

3. Sew the blocks, sashing units, and side setting triangles together into rows; press.

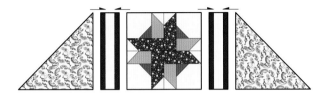

4. Sew the sashing units, sashing squares, and sashing triangles together into rows; press.

5. Sew the block rows and sashing rows together; press the seams toward the sashing rows. Add the paisley half-square triangles last. Press the seams toward the paisley triangles.

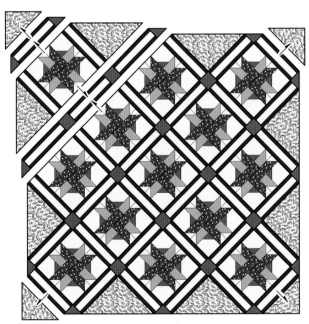

Assembly diagram

6. To trim and straighten the quilt top, align the ¼" mark on your ruler with the outermost points of the blocks. Use a rotary cutter to trim any excess fabric, leaving a ¼"-wide seam allowance. Square the corners of the quilt top as necessary.

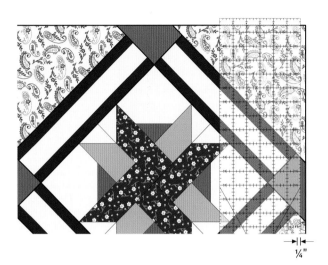

¼"

Adding the Borders

For detailed instructions, refer to "Borders" on page 17.

1. Measure, cut, and sew seven of the 2"-wide navy tonal inner-border strips to the quilt top.

2. To make the flat piping, join the 1"-wide red strips end to end to make a continuous strip. Fold the long strip in half lengthwise, wrong sides together, and press. Measure the quilt through the center from top to bottom and cut two strips from the long strip to fit that measurement.

3. Position the raw edges of the cut piping even with the quilt edges. Baste the strips to the side edges of the quilt top using a scant ¼" seam allowance.

4. Measure the quilt through the center from side to side and cut two red strips from the remainder of the long strip to fit that measurement.

5. Position the raw edges of the cut piping even with the quilt edges. Baste the strips to the top and bottom edges of the quilt top, overlapping the strips in the corners.

6. Measure, cut, and sew the 8½"-wide floral outer-border strips to the quilt top.

Finishing the Quilt

For detailed instructions on the following techniques, refer to "Finishing Your Quilt" on page 19.

1. Cut and piece the backing fabric so it is 4" to 6" larger than the quilt top. Layer the quilt top with batting and backing. Baste the layers together.

2. Hand or machine quilt as desired. You may wish to quilt a continuous design over the center of the quilt. Quilt a wavy line in the inner border and a continuous design of small and large loops in the outer border.

3. Square up the quilt sandwich.

4. Add a hanging sleeve, if desired.

5. Using the remaining 2"-wide navy tonal strips, sew the binding to the quilt. Add a label, if desired.

Square CROSSING

I love using red and black fabrics to create a dramatic effect. In this striking quilt, several red tonal prints and black tonal prints are used to add visual interest. You could use just two prints; the key is that they contrast with the background to carry the design.

Finished Quilt Size: 62" x 74"
Finished Block Size: 12"

Materials

Yardages are based on 42″-wide fabrics.

2 yards of red-and-black floral for outer border
½ yard *each* of 4 assorted red tonal prints for blocks
1½ yards of cream background print for blocks
½ yard *each* of 3 assorted black tonal prints for blocks
1⅓ yards of black tonal print for blocks, inner border, and binding
4¼ yards of fabric for backing
67" x 79" piece of batting

Cutting

All measurements include ¼″-wide seam allowances. Cut all strips across the width of the fabric (selvage to selvage) unless instructed otherwise.

From *each* of the 4 assorted red tonal prints, cut:
2 strips (8 total), 4½" x 42"; crosscut into 40 squares, 4½" x 4½"
2 strips (8 total), 2½" x 42"

From *each* of the 3 assorted black tonal prints, cut:
2 strips (6 total), 4½" x 42"; crosscut into 30 squares, 4½" x 4½"
2 strips (6 total), 2½" x 42"

From the black tonal print for blocks, inner border, and binding, cut:
2 strips, 4½" x 42"; crosscut into 10 squares, 4½" x 4½"
2 strips, 2½" x 42"
8 strips, 2" x 42"
6 strips, 1½" x 42"

From the cream background print, cut:
5 strips, 4½" x 42"; crosscut into 80 rectangles, 2½" x 4½"
10 strips, 2½" x 42"; crosscut into 160 squares, 2½" x 2½"

From the *lengthwise grain* of the red-and-black floral, cut:
4 strips, 6½" x 65"

Making the Blocks

1. Refer to "Making Strip Sets" on page 11. Sew one 2½" x 42" red strip and one 2½" x 42" black strip together to make a strip set. Press toward the black strip. Make two strip sets from the same black-and-red fabric combination. Make a total of eight strip sets. Cut the strips into 2½"-wide segments. Crosscut each strip set into 15 segments. Keep the segments from the same combination of fabrics together.

2½"

Make 2 matching strip sets (8 total).
Cut 15 segments from each (120 total).

2. Sew two segments from the same combination of fabrics together to make a four-patch unit; press. Refer to "Four-Patch Units" on page 15 for guidance on positioning and pressing the center seam allowance. Make 20 units.

Make 20.

3. Sew one segment from step 1 and one 2½" x 4½" cream rectangle together as shown to make a side unit; press. Make 40 side units and 40 reversed side units.

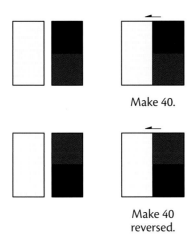

Make 40.

Make 40 reversed.

4. Using the square-on-square-unit technique on page 12, draw a diagonal line from corner to corner on the wrong side of the 2½" cream squares. Sew two cream squares to opposite corners of one 4½" black square as shown to make a corner unit; press. Make 40 units. You'll have 80 cream squares left over for the next step.

Make 40.

5. Sew two cream squares from step 4 to opposite corners of one 4½" red square as shown to make a corner unit; press. Make 40 units.

Make 40.

6. Sew one four-patch unit from step 2, two side units and two reversed side units from the same combination of fabrics from step 3, two corner units from step 4, and two corner units from step 5 together as shown to make a block. Make 20 blocks. Press 10 blocks as shown and label them block A. Press the remaining 10 blocks as shown and label them block B.

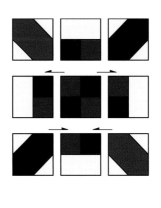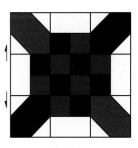

Block A.
Make 10.

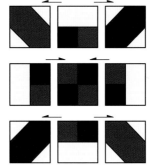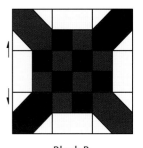

Block B.
Make 10.

Assembling the Quilt Top

For detailed instructions, refer to "Quilts with Blocks Set Side by Side" on page 16.

1. Arrange the blocks into five horizontal rows of four blocks each as shown in the assembly diagram below, alternating blocks A and B in each row.

2. Sew the blocks into rows. Press the seams in alternate directions from row to row. Stitch the rows together. Press the seams in one direction.

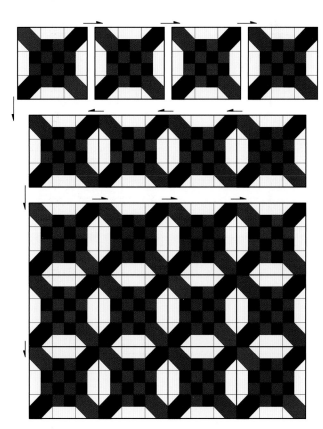

Assembly diagram

3. Refer to "Borders" on page 17. Measure, cut, and sew the 1½"-wide black inner-border strips and then the 6½"-wide floral outer-border strips to the quilt top.

Finishing the Quilt

For detailed instructions on the following techniques, refer to "Finishing Your Quilt" on page 19.

1. Cut and piece the backing fabric so it is 4" to 6" larger than the quilt top. Layer the quilt top with batting and backing. Baste the layers together.

2. Hand or machine quilt as desired. You may wish to quilt diagonal lines through the blocks in both directions, and additional diagonal lines through the squares. Quilt straight lines in the inner and outer borders.

3. Square up the quilt sandwich.

4. Add a hanging sleeve, if desired.

5. Using the 2"-wide black tonal strips, sew the binding to the quilt. Add a label, if desired.

Ice CRYSTALS

The snowflake print in the outer border and the monochromatic palette are a perfect choice for this striking winter-themed quilt. You'll be amazed how quickly the blocks zoom together using sew-and-trim techniques.

Finished Quilt Size: 71" x 89"
Finished Block Size: 16"

Materials

Yardages are based on 42″-wide fabrics.

2⅜ yards of blue snowflake print for outer border

2 yards of navy print for blocks, inner border, and binding

1⅔ yards of light blue fern print for blocks and sashing

1⅜ yards of white background print for blocks

⅔ yard of medium blue tonal print for blocks and sashing corners

⅝ yard of royal blue tonal print for sashing

6 yards of fabric for backing

76" x 94" piece of batting

Cutting

All measurements include ¼″-wide seam allowances. Cut all strips across the width of the fabric (selvage to selvage) unless instructed otherwise.

From the navy print, cut:
2 strips, 4½" x 42"
10 strips, 2½" x 42"; crosscut *6 strips* into 96 squares, 2½" x 2½"
16 strips, 2" x 42"

From the white background print, cut:
3 strips, 8½" x 42"; crosscut into 48 rectangles, 2½" x 8½"
2 strips, 4½" x 42"
4 strips, 2½" x 42"

From the medium blue tonal print, cut:
2 strips, 2½" x 42"
1 strip, 2½" x 42"; crosscut into 2 pieces, 2½" x 21"
5 strips, 2½" x 42"; crosscut into 68 squares, 2½" x 2½"

From the light blue fern print, cut:
1 strip, 12½" x 42"
1 strip, 12½" x 42"; crosscut into:
   1 piece, 12½" x 21"
   8 rectangles, 2½" x 12½"
1 strip, 12½" x 42"; crosscut into 16 rectangles, 2½" x 12½"
2 strips, 8½" x 42"

From the royal blue tonal print, cut:
4 strips, 4½" x 42"

From the *lengthwise grain* of the blue snowflake print, cut:
4 strips, 6½" x 80"

Making the Blocks

1. Refer to "Making Strip Sets" on page 11. Sew one 4½" x 42" navy strip between two 2½" x 42" white strips to make a strip set. Press toward the navy strip. Make two. Cut the strip sets into 4½"-wide segments. Cut 12 segments.

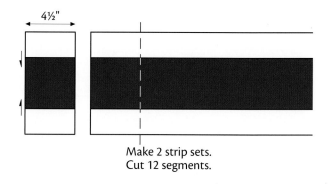

Make 2 strip sets.
Cut 12 segments.

2. Sew one 4½" x 42" white strip between two 2½" x 42" navy strips to make a strip set. Press toward the navy strips. Make two. Cut the strip sets into 2½"-wide segments. Cut 24 segments.

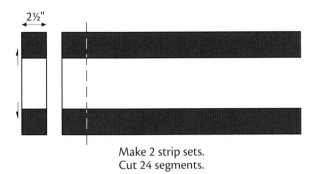

2½"

Make 2 strip sets.
Cut 24 segments.

3. Sew one segment from step 1 between two segments from step 2 to make a center unit as shown; press. Make 12 units.

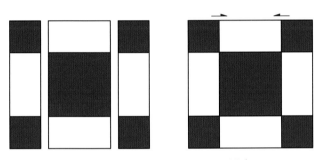

Make 12.

4. Using the square-and-rectangle-unit technique on page 12, draw a diagonal line from corner to corner on the wrong side of the 2½" navy squares. Sew a navy square on opposite ends of an 8½" white rectangle as shown; press. Make 48 units.

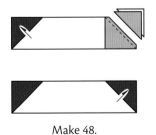

Make 48.

5. Sew one center unit from step 3, four units from step 4, and four 2½" medium blue squares together as shown; press. Make 12 units.

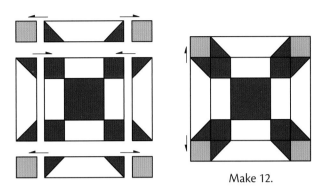

Make 12.

6. Sew one 12½" x 42" fern print strip between two 2½" x 42" medium blue strips to make a strip set. Sew one 12½" x 21" fern print piece between two 2½" x 21" medium blue pieces to make a short strip set. Press toward the fern print strips. Cut the strip sets into 2½"-wide segments. Cut a total of 24 segments.

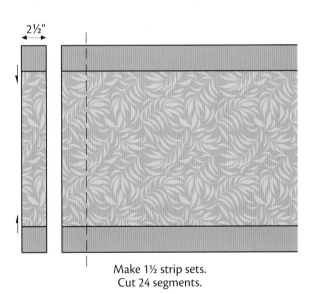

2½"

Make 1½ strip sets.
Cut 24 segments.

7. Sew one unit from step 5, two segments from step 6, and two 2½" x 12½" fern print rectangles together as shown to make a block; press. Make 12 blocks.

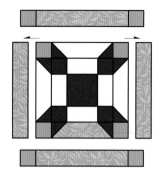
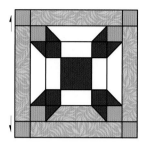

Make 12.

Assembling the Quilt Top

For detailed instructions, refer to "Quilts with Sashing Strips" on page 16.

1. Refer to "Making Strip Sets" on page 11. Sew one 8½" x 42" fern print strip between two 4½" x 42" royal blue strips to make a strip set. Press toward the royal blue strips. Make two. Cut the strip sets into 2½"-wide segments. Cut 31 segments.

2½"

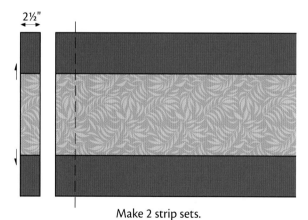

Make 2 strip sets.
Cut 31 segments.

2. Arrange and sew together four segments from step 1 and three blocks, alternating them as shown to make a block row; press. Make four rows.

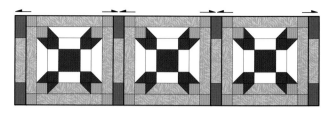

Make 4.

3. Arrange and sew together three segments from step 1 and four 2½" medium blue squares as shown to make a sashing row; press. Make five rows.

Make 5.

4. Sew the block rows and sashing rows together, alternating them as shown in the assembly diagram. Press the seams toward the sashing rows.

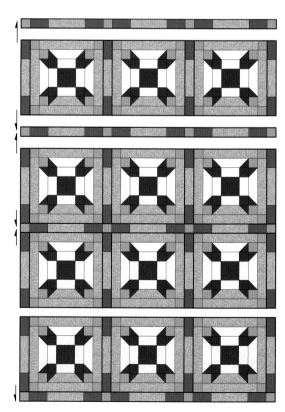

Assembly diagram

5. Refer to "Borders" on page 17. Measure, cut, and sew seven of the 2"-wide navy inner-border strips and then the 6½"-wide snowflake outer-border strips to the quilt top.

Finishing the Quilt

For detailed instructions on the following techniques, refer to "Finishing Your Quilt" on page 19.

1. Cut and piece the backing fabric so it is 4" to 6" larger than the quilt top. Layer the quilt top with batting and backing. Baste the layers together.

2. Hand or machine quilt as desired. You may wish to quilt a medallion in the center of the blocks and a smaller medallion over the sashing corners. Quilt curvy, meandering lines over the light blue areas and a continuous design in the inner border and outer border.

3. Square up the quilt sandwich.

4. Add a hanging sleeve, if desired.

5. Using the remaining 2"-wide navy strips, sew the binding to the quilt. Add a label, if desired.

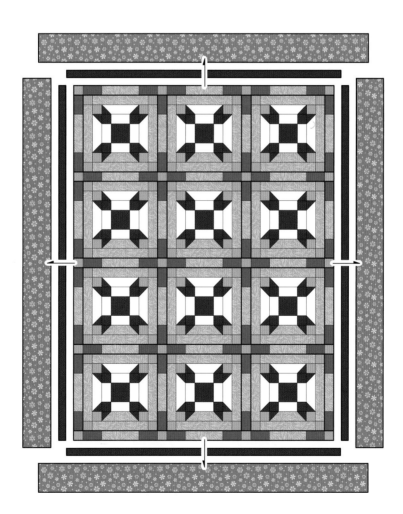

Pinwheel PUZZLE

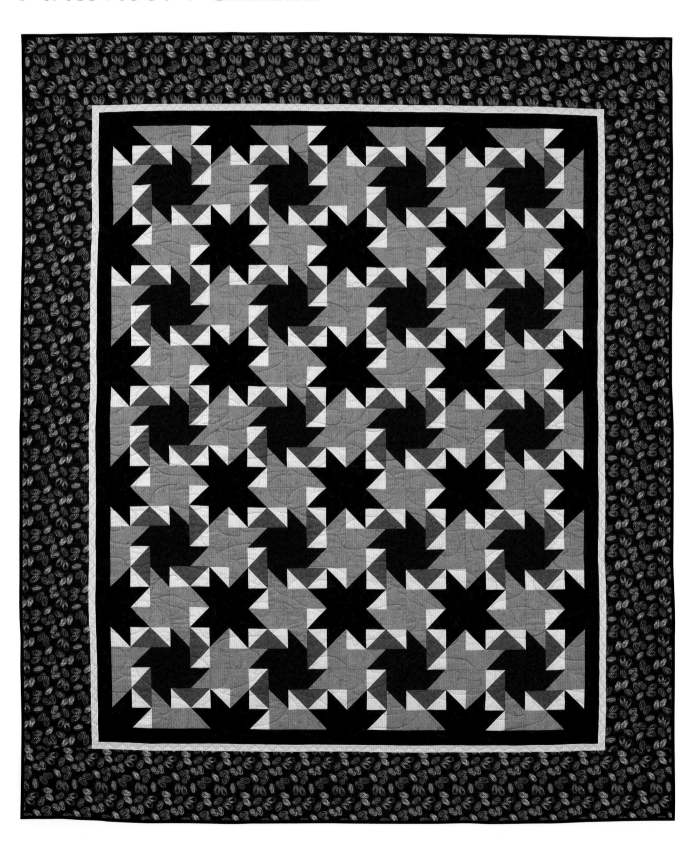

The intriguing block in this quilt may have the look of a puzzle, but set the blocks together and fantastic dark stars come into view. The red and blue prints lend a patriotic mood to this wonderful quilt, while the border print adds a bit of whimsy.

Finished Quilt Size: 66" x 78"
Finished Block Size: 12"

Materials

Yardages are based on 42″-wide fabrics.

2⅛ yards of navy novelty print for outer border
2 yards of navy tonal print for blocks, inner border, and binding
1⅜ yards of vanilla cream print for blocks and middle border
1⅜ yards of tan tonal print for blocks
⅞ yard of blue tonal print for blocks
¾ yard of red tonal print for blocks
5¼ yards of fabric for backing
71" x 83" piece of batting

Cutting

All measurements include ¼″-wide seam allowances. Cut all strips across the width of the fabric (selvage to selvage) unless instructed otherwise.

From the vanilla cream print, cut:
15 strips, 2½" x 42"; crosscut into 240 squares, 2½" x 2½"
6 strips, 1¼" x 42"

From the blue tonal print, cut:
5 strips, 5¼" x 42"; crosscut into 40 rectangles, 4½" x 5¼"

From the navy tonal print, cut:
5 strips, 4½" x 42"; crosscut into 80 rectangles, 2½" x 4½"
5 strips, 2½" x 42"; crosscut into 80 squares, 2½" x 2½"
14 strips, 2" x 42"

From the tan tonal print, cut:
10 strips, 4½" x 42"; crosscut into 160 rectangles, 2½" x 4½"

From the red tonal print, cut:
5 strips, 4½" x 42"; crosscut into 80 rectangles, 2½" x 4½"

From the *lengthwise grain* of the navy novelty print, cut:
4 strips, 7¼" x 69"

Making the Blocks

1. Using the flying-geese-unit technique on page 14, draw a diagonal line from corner to corner on the wrong side of the 2½" cream squares. Sew four cream squares to each blue rectangle as shown; press. Cut 80 flying-geese units as instructed. You'll have 80 cream squares left over to use in step 3.

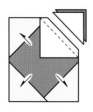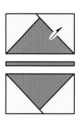

Make 80.

2. Using the square-and-rectangle-unit technique on page 12, draw a diagonal line from corner to corner on the wrong side of the 2½" navy squares. Sew one navy square to one end of a tan rectangle as shown; press. Make 80 units.

Make 80.

3. Using the square-and-rectangle-unit technique and the marked squares from step 1, sew a cream square to one end of a navy rectangle as shown; press. Make 80 units.

Make 80.

4. Using the rectangle-to-rectangle-unit technique on page 13, draw a diagonal line on the wrong side of the remaining 2½" x 4½" tan rectangles. Sew a tan rectangle to one end of a red rectangle as shown; press. Make 80 units.

Make 80.

5. Sew one unit from step 1 and one unit from step 2 together as shown; press. Make 80.

Make 80.

6. Sew one unit from step 3 and one unit from step 5 together as shown; press. Make 80.

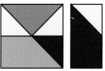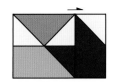

Make 80.

7. Sew one unit from step 4 and one unit from step 6 together as shown to make a unit; press. Make 80 units.

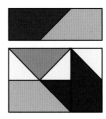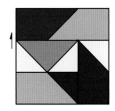

Make 80.

8. Sew four units from step 7 together, rotating the units 90° as shown to make a block; press. Refer to "Four-Patch Units" on page 15 for guidance on positioning and pressing the center seam allowance. Make 20 blocks.

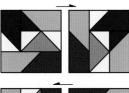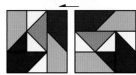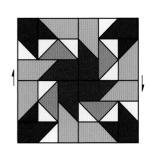

Make 20.

Assembling the Quilt Top

For detailed instructions, refer to "Quilts with Blocks Set Side by Side" on page 16.

1. Arrange the blocks into five horizontal rows of four blocks each as shown in the assembly diagram below.

2. Sew the blocks into rows. Press the seams in alternate directions from row to row. Stitch the rows together. Press the seams in one direction.

Assembly diagram

3. Refer to "Borders" on page 17. Measure, cut, and sew six of the 2"-wide navy tonal inner-border strips, then the 1¼"-wide cream middle-border strips, and lastly the 7¼"-wide novelty outer-border strips to the quilt top.

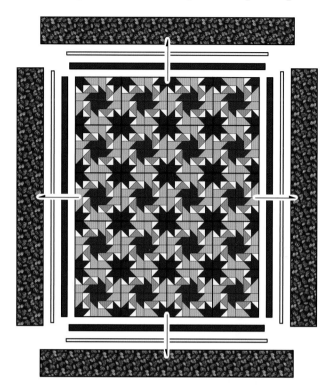

Finishing the Quilt

For detailed instructions on the following techniques, refer to "Finishing Your Quilt" on page 19.

1. Cut and piece the backing fabric so it is 4" to 6" larger than the quilt top. Layer the quilt top with batting and backing. Baste the layers together.

2. Hand or machine quilt as desired. You may wish to quilt a continuous design over the center of the quilt. Quilt a small zigzag design over the middle border and a continuous geometric design in the outer border.

3. Square up the quilt sandwich.

4. Add a hanging sleeve, if desired.

5. Using the remaining 2"-wide navy tonal strips, sew the binding to the quilt. Add a label, if desired.

Summer STARS

Squares and rectangles are all you'll need to make these charming Star blocks; they're so quick and easy. The timeless combination of blue and yellow fabrics will remind you of summer all year long.

Finished Quilt Size: 64" x 64"
Finished Block Size: 12"

Materials

Yardages are based on 42˝-wide fabrics. Fat quarters measure 18˝ x 21˝.

2 yards of large-scale floral print for outer border

1⅜ yards of small-scale floral print for setting blocks and triangles

1⅛ yards of dark blue print for blocks and binding

1⅛ yards of cream background print for blocks

½ yard of yellow print for blocks

½ yard of yellow-and-orange stripe for inner border

⅓ yard of light blue print for blocks

1 fat quarter of blue floral print for blocks

4¼ yards of fabric for backing

69" x 69" piece of batting

Cutting

All measurements include ¼˝-wide seam allowances. Cut all strips across the width of the fabric (selvage to selvage) unless instructed otherwise.

From the cream background print, cut:

5 strips, 2½" x 42"; crosscut into 36 rectangles, 2½" x 4½"

5 strips, 2½" x 42"; crosscut into 72 squares, 2½" x 2½"

3 strips, 2½" x 42"

From the light blue print, cut:

3 strips, 2½" x 42"

From the yellow print, cut:

5 strips, 2½" x 42"; crosscut into 72 squares, 2½" x 2½"

From the dark blue print, cut:

9 strips, 2½" x 42"; crosscut into 72 rectangles, 2½" x 4½"

7 strips, 2" x 42"

From the blue floral print, cut:

9 squares, 4½" x 4½"

From the small-scale floral print, cut:

2 squares, 18½" x 18½"; cut twice diagonally to yield 8 side triangles

4 squares, 12½" x 12½"

2 squares, 9½" x 9½"; cut once diagonally to yield 4 corner triangles

From the yellow-and-orange stripe, cut:

6 strips, 2" x 42"

From the *lengthwise grain* of the large-scale floral print, cut:

4 strips, 5½" x 67"

Making the Blocks

1. Refer to "Making Strip Sets" on page 11. Sew one 2½" x 42" cream strip and one 2½" x 42" light blue strip together to make a strip set. Press toward the light blue strip. Make three. Cut the strip sets into 2½"-wide segments. Cut 36 segments.

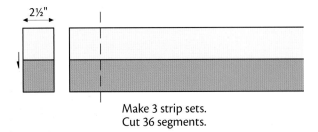

2½"

Make 3 strip sets.
Cut 36 segments.

2. Sew one segment from step 1 and one 2½" x 4½" cream rectangle together as shown to make a corner unit. Make 36 units.

Make 36.

3. Using the parallelogram-unit technique on page 14, draw a diagonal line from corner to corner on the wrong side of the 2½" cream squares and 2½" yellow squares. Stitch a cream square and a yellow square to a dark blue rectangle as shown. Press as indicated. Make 36 and label them unit A. You'll use the remaining marked squares in the next step.

Unit A.
Make 36.

4. Repeat step 3 to make a reverse unit. Press as indicated. Make 36 and label them unit B.

Unit B.
Make 36.

5. Sew one of unit A and one of unit B together as shown to make a side unit; press. Make 36.

Make 36.

6. Sew four corner units from step 2, four side units from step 5, and one 4½" blue floral square together as shown to make a block; press. Make nine blocks.

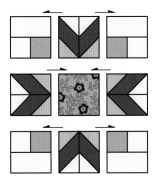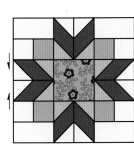

Make 9.

Assembling the Quilt Top

For detailed instructions, refer to "Quilts Set Diagonally" on page 17. The setting triangles have been cut slightly oversized. You will trim them after the quilt center is assembled.

1. Lay out the Star blocks and 12½" setting squares. Add the side triangles.

2. Sew the blocks, setting squares, and side tri-angles together into rows, pressing toward the floral print.

3. Sew the rows together, adding the corner tri-angles last. Press the seams toward the floral print.

Assembly diagram

4. To trim and straighten the quilt top, align the ¼" mark on your ruler with the outermost points of the blocks. Use a rotary cutter to trim any excess fabric, leaving a ¼"-wide seam allowance. Square the corners of the quilt top as necessary.

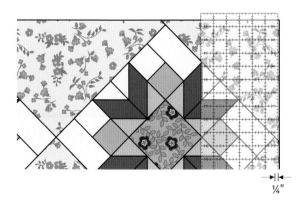

¼"

5. Refer to "Borders" on page 17. Measure, cut, and sew the 2"-wide striped inner-border strips and then the 5½"-wide floral outer-border strips to the quilt top.

Finishing the Quilt

For detailed instructions on the following tech-niques, refer to "Finishing Your Quilt" on page 19.

1. Cut and piece the backing fabric so it is 4" to 6" larger than the quilt top. Layer the quilt top with batting and backing. Baste the layers together.

2. Hand or machine quilt as desired. You may wish to quilt a medallion in the center of the blocks and in the background squares, as well as a partial medallion in the large setting tri-angles. Quilt a continuous loop design in the inner border and a continuous design in the outer border.

3. Square up the quilt sandwich.

4. Add a hanging sleeve, if desired.

5. Using the 2"-wide dark blue strips, sew the binding to the quilt. Add a label, if desired.

Tulip BOUQUET

Celebrate the arrival of spring with this sweet quilt. I love red tulips, but you can make your tulips any color—just be sure to use many different prints. Then gather a variety of green prints, and you're all set to make this cheerful quilt.

Finished Quilt Size: 60½" x 60½"
Finished Block Size: 13"

Materials

Yardages are based on 42˝-wide fabrics. Fat quarters measure 18˝ x 21˝.

2 yards of floral print for outer border and binding

1⅞ yards of cream tonal print for blocks, sashing, and inner border

1 fat quarter *each* of 6 assorted red tonal prints for blocks

1 fat quarter *each* of 6 assorted green tonal prints for blocks

½ yard of dark green tonal print for blocks

⅜ yard of yellow tonal print for blocks and middle border

4 yards of fabric for backing

66" x 66" piece of batting

Cutting

All measurements include ¼˝-wide seam allowances. Cut all strips across the width of the fabric (selvage to selvage) unless instructed otherwise.

From the cream tonal print, cut:

5 strips, 5¼" x 42"; crosscut into 36 rectangles, 4½" x 5¼"

3 strips, 2½" x 42"; crosscut into 6 rectangles, 2½" x 13½"

7 strips, 2½" x 42"

2 strips, 2½" x 42"; crosscut into 36 rectangles, 1½" x 2½"

2 strips, 1½" x 42"

From the yellow tonal print, cut:

2 strips, 1½" x 42"

5 strips, 1¼" x 42"

From *each* of the 6 assorted red prints, cut:

3 strips (18 total), 2½" x 21"; crosscut into 108 squares, 2½" x 2½"

From *each* of the 6 assorted green prints, cut:

4 strips (24 total), 2½" x 21"; crosscut into 180 squares, 2½" x 2½"

From the dark green tonal print, cut:

5 strips, 1½" x 42"; crosscut into 9 rectangles, 1½" x 13½"

3 strips, 1½" x 42"; crosscut into 18 rectangles, 1½" x 6½"

From the *lengthwise grain* of the floral print, cut:

4 strips, 6½" x 63"

5 strips, 2" x 52"

Making the Blocks

1. Refer to "Making Strip Sets" on page 11. Sew one 1½" x 42" cream strip and one 1½" x 42" yellow strip together to make a strip set. Press toward the yellow strip. Make two. Cut the strip sets into 1½"-wide segments. Cut 36 segments.

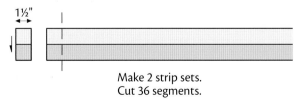

Make 2 strip sets.
Cut 36 segments.

2. Sew one segment from step 1 and one 1½" x 2½" cream rectangle together as shown to make a corner unit; press. Make 36 units.

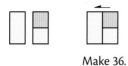

Make 36.

3. Using the flying-geese-unit technique on page 14, draw a diagonal line from corner to corner on the wrong side of 72 of the 2½" assorted red squares and 72 of the 2½" assorted green squares. Sew two red squares and two green squares to one 4½" x 5¼" cream rectangle as shown; press. Cut the units as instructed. Make 36 flying-geese units and 36 reverse flying-geese units.

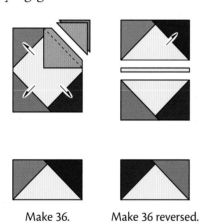

Make 36.   Make 36 reversed.

4. Sew one 2½" assorted red square and three 2½" assorted green squares together to make a four-patch unit; press. Refer to "Four-Patch Units" on page 15 for guidance on positioning and pressing the center seam allowance. Make 36 units.

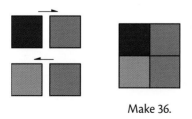

Make 36.

5. Sew one unit from step 2, one flying-geese unit and one reverse flying-geese unit from step 3, and one four-patch unit from step 4 together as shown to make a large corner unit; press. Make 36 units.

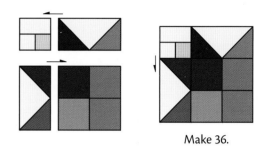

Make 36.

6. Sew four units from step 5, two 1½" x 6½" dark green rectangles, and one 1½" x 13½" dark green rectangle together as shown to make a block; press. Make nine blocks.

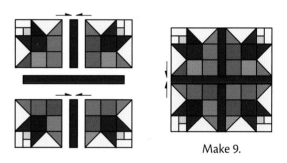

Make 9.

Assembling the Quilt Top

For detailed instructions, refer to "Quilts with Sashing Strips" on page 16.

1. Arrange and sew together two 2½" x 13½" cream sashing units and three blocks, alternating them as shown to make a block row; press. Make three rows.

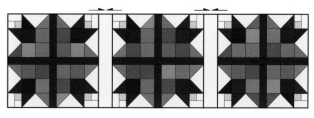

Make 3.

2. Measure the length of each of the three block rows. If they differ, calculate the average and consider this the length. Sew the 2½" x 42" cream strips together end to end to make a continuous strip. From this long strip, cut two sashing strips the length of your row measurement. You'll need the rest of the long strip for the inner border.

3. Sew the block rows and the two sashing strips from step 2 together, alternating them as shown in the assembly diagram. Press the seams toward the sashing strips.

Assembly diagram

4. Refer to "Borders" on page 17. Measure, cut, and sew the remaining 2½"-wide cream strip from step 2 for the inner border, then the 1¼"-wide yellow tonal middle-border strips, and

lastly the 6½"-wide floral outer-border strips to the quilt top.

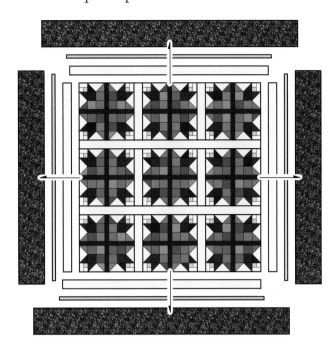

Finishing the Quilt

For detailed instructions on the following techniques, refer to "Finishing Your Quilt" on page 19.

1. Cut and piece the backing fabric so it is 4" to 6" larger than the quilt top. Layer the quilt top with batting and backing. Baste the layers together.

2. Hand or machine quilt as desired. You may wish to quilt a medallion in the center of the blocks. Quilt loops and leaves in the sashing and a small continuous loop in the inner border. Quilt a continuous leaf design in the outer border.

3. Square up the quilt sandwich.

4. Add a hanging sleeve, if desired.

5. Using the 2"-wide floral strips, sew the binding to the quilt. Add a label, if desired.

Star CROSS

This delightful quilt is perfect for anyone who loves boats and sailing. The blocks are super easy to make, and the sashing intersections resemble knots or cork floats, adding to the nautical theme. Kids of all ages will love this design!

Finished Quilt Size: 55" x 65½"
Finished Block Size: 9"

Materials

Yardages are based on 42˝-wide fabrics.

1¾ yards of navy nautical print for outer border and binding

1⅓ yards of cream print for blocks

1¼ yards of navy tonal print for blocks, sashing, and inner border

⅔ yard of royal blue tonal print for blocks

⅝ yard of red print for blocks, sashing squares, and middle border

3¾ yards of fabric for backing

60" x 71" piece of batting

Cutting

All measurements include ¼˝-wide seam allowances. Cut all strips across the width of the fabric (selvage to selvage) unless instructed otherwise.

From the red print, cut:

4 strips, 2" x 42"; crosscut into 80 squares, 2" x 2"

1 rectangle, 2" x 26"

5 strips, 1¼" x 42"

From the navy tonal print, cut:

1 strip, 9½" x 42"; crosscut into 19 rectangles, 2" x 9½"

1 rectangle, 9½" x 26"

4 strips, 2" x 42"; crosscut into 80 squares, 2" x 2"

5 strips, 2" x 42"

From the cream print, cut:

10 strips, 3½" x 42"; crosscut into 80 rectangles, 3½" x 5"

4 strips, 2" x 42"; crosscut into 80 squares, 2" x 2"

From the royal blue tonal print, cut:

4 strips, 5" x 42"; crosscut into 80 rectangles, 2" x 5"

From the *lengthwise grain* of the navy nautical print, cut:

4 strips, 5½" x 58"

5 strips, 2" x 51"

Making the Blocks

1. Using the square-and-rectangle-unit technique on page 12, draw a diagonal line from corner to corner on the wrong side of the 2" red squares and 2" navy squares. Sew one red square and one navy square to opposite corners of a 3½" x 5" cream rectangle as shown; press. Make 80 units.

Make 80.

2. Using the square-and-rectangle-unit technique, draw a diagonal line from corner to corner on the wrong side of the 2" cream squares. Sew a cream square to one end of a royal blue rectangle as shown; press. Make 80 units.

Make 80.

3. Sew one unit from step 1 and one unit from step 2 together as shown to make a corner unit; press. Make 80 units.

Make 80.

4. Sew four units from step 3 together, rotating the units 90° as shown to make a block; press. Refer to "Four-Patch Units" on page 15 for guidance on positioning and pressing the center seam allowance. Make 20 blocks.

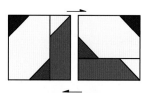

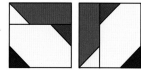

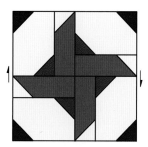

Make 20.

Assembling the Quilt Top

For detailed instructions, refer to "Quilts with Sashing Strips" on page 16.

1. Refer to "Making Strip Sets" on page 11. Sew one 2" x 26" red rectangle and one 9½" x 26" navy tonal rectangle together to make a strip set. Press toward the navy rectangle. Cut the strip set into 2"-wide segments. Cut 12 segments.

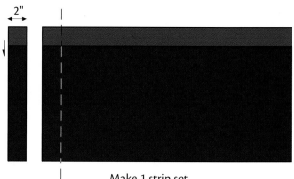

Make 1 strip set.
Cut 12 segments.

2. Arrange and sew together three 2" x 9½" navy tonal rectangles and four blocks, alternating them as shown to make a block row; press. Make five rows.

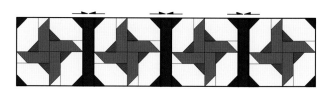

Make 5.

3. Arrange and sew together three segments from step 1 and one 2" x 9½" navy tonal rectangle as shown to make a sashing row; press. Make four rows.

Make 4.

4. Sew the block rows and sashing rows together, alternating them as shown in the assembly diagram. Press the seams toward the sashing rows.

Assembly diagram

5. Refer to "Borders" on page 17. Measure, cut, and sew the 2"-wide navy tonal inner-border strips, then the 1¼"-wide red middle-border strips, and lastly the 5½"-wide nautical print outer-border strips to the quilt top.

Finishing the Quilt

For detailed instructions on the following techniques, refer to "Finishing Your Quilt" on page 19.

1. Cut and piece the backing fabric so it is 4" to 6" larger than the quilt top. Layer the quilt top with batting and backing. Baste the layers together.

2. Hand or machine quilt as desired. You may wish to quilt a medallion in the center of the blocks and a small continuous star-and-loops design over the sashing and inner border. Quilt a small continuous loop over the middle border and a larger continuous star-and-loops design in the outer border.

3. Square up the quilt sandwich.

4. Add a hanging sleeve, if desired.

5. Using the 2"-wide nautical print strips, sew the binding to the quilt. Add a label, if desired.

About the AUTHOR

Author, teacher, fabric designer, and award-winning quiltmaker, Nancy Mahoney has enjoyed making quilts for more than 20 years. An impressive range of her beautiful quilts have been featured in many national and international quilt magazines.

Square Deal is Nancy's seventh book with Martingale & Company. Her other bestselling books include *Quilt Revival* (2006), *Quilt Block Bonanza: 50 Paper-Pieced Designs* (2005), and *Patchwork Showcase* (2004).

Almost entirely self-taught, Nancy continues to explore new ways to combine traditional blocks and updated techniques to create quilts that are fun and easy to make.

Nancy lives in Florida with her life partner of 30 years, Tom, and their umbrella cockatoo, Prince.

New and Bestselling Titles from

America's Best-Loved Craft & Hobby Books®
America's Best-Loved Knitting Books®

America's Best-Loved Quilt Books®

APPLIQUÉ
Adoration Quilts
Appliqué at Play *NEW!*
Appliqué Takes Wing
Easy Appliqué Samplers
Favorite Quilts
     from Anka's Treasures *NEW!*
Garden Party
Mimi Dietrich's Baltimore Basics *NEW!*
Raise the Roof
Stitch and Split Appliqué
Tea in the Garden

FOCUS ON WOOL
Hooked on Wool
Purely Primitive
Simply Primitive
Warm Up to Wool

GENERAL QUILTMAKING
All Buttoned Up *NEW!*
Alphabet Soup
American Doll Quilts
Calendar Kids *NEW!*
Cottage-Style Quilts
Creating Your Perfect Quilting Space
Creative Quilt Collection Volume One
Dazzling Quilts *NEW!*
Follow the Dots . . . to Dazzling Quilts
Follow-the-Line Quilting Designs
Follow-the-Line Quilting Designs
     Volume Two
Fresh Look at Seasonal Quilts, A *NEW!*
Merry Christmas Quilts
Prairie Children and Their Quilts *NEW!*
Primitive Gatherings
Quilt Revival
Sensational Sashiko
Simple Traditions

LEARNING TO QUILT
Blessed Home Quilt, The
Happy Endings, Revised Edition
Let's Quilt!
Magic of Quiltmaking, The
Quilter's Quick Reference Guide, The
Your First Quilt Book (or it should be!)

PAPER PIECING
40 Bright and Bold Paper-Pieced Blocks
300 Paper-Pieced Quilt Blocks
Easy Machine Paper Piecing
Quilt Block Bonanza
Quilter's Ark, A
Show Me How to Paper Piece
Spellbinding Quilts *NEW!*

PIECING
40 Fabulous Quick-Cut Quilts
101 Fabulous Rotary-Cut Quilts
365 Quilt Blocks a Year: Perpetual Calendar
1000 Great Quilt Blocks
Better by the Dozen
Big 'n Easy
Border Workbook, 10th Anniversary
     Edition, The *NEW!*
Clever Quarters, Too *NEW!*
Lickety-Split Quilts
New Cuts for New Quilts *NEW!*
Over Easy
Sew One and You're Done
Simple Chenille Quilts
Snowball Quilts *NEW!*
Stack a New Deck
Sudoku Quilts *NEW!*
Two-Block Theme Quilts
Twosey-Foursey Quilts *NEW!*
Variations on a Theme
Wheel of Mystery Quilts

QUILTS FOR BABIES & CHILDREN
Even More Quilts for Baby
More Quilts for Baby
Quilts for Baby
Sweet and Simple Baby Quilts

SCRAP QUILTS
More Nickel Quilts
Nickel Quilts
Save the Scraps
Scraps of Time
Simple Strategies for Scrap Quilts *NEW!*
Successful Scrap Quilts from
     Simple Rectangles
Treasury of Scrap Quilts, A

CRAFTS
Bag Boutique
Greeting Cards Using Digital Photos
It's a Wrap
Miniature Punchneedle Embroidery
Passion for Punchneedle, A *NEW!*
Scrapbooking Off the Page…and on
     the Wall

KNITTING & CROCHET
365 Knitting Stitches a Year:
     Perpetual Calendar
Crochet from the Heart
Cute Crochet for Kids *NEW!*
First Crochet
First Knits
Fun and Funky Crochet
Funky Chunky Knitted Accessories
Handknit Style II *NEW!*
Knits from the Heart
Knits, Knots, Buttons, and Bows
Knitter's Book of Finishing Techniques, The
Little Box of Crocheted Hats and Scarves,
     The
Little Box of Knitted Throws, The
Little Box of Scarves, The
Modern Classics *NEW!*
Pursenalities
Saturday Sweaters
Sensational Knitted Socks
Silk Knits *NEW!*
Yarn Stash Workbook, The

Our books are available at
bookstores and your favorite
craft, fabric, and yarn retailers.
If you don't see the title
you're looking for, visit us at
www.martingale-pub.com
or contact us at:
1-800-426-3126

International: 1-425-483-3313
Fax: 1-425-486-7596
Email: info@martingale-pub.com